THE UNITED STATES MARINES

A Pictorial History

Books by Lynn Montross

WAR THROUGH THE AGES

THE RELUCTANT REBELS

RAG, TAG AND BOBTAIL

CAVALRY OF THE SKY

WASHINGTON AND THE AMERICAN REVOLUTION (teen-age)

U. S. MARINE OPERATIONS IN KOREA

First, second and third volumes with Captain Nicholas A. Canzona, USMC; fourth volume with Major William T. Hickman, USMC, and Major Hubard D. Kuokka, USMC; fifth and final volume in preparation.

THE UNITED STATES MARINES: A Pictorial History

THE UNITED STATES MARINES

by Lynn Montross

A Pictorial History

Introduction by
Senator Paul H. Douglas

Photographic Research by
Captain David E. Schwulst, USMCR

BRAMHALL HOUSE, New York

This edition is published by Bramhall House,
a division of Clarkson N. Potter, Inc.,
by arrangement with the original publishers,
Holt, Rinehart & Winston, Inc.

(D)

INTRODUCTION

This is the story of a Corps which, in our country's service, has always scorned ease and instead sought danger. It is the story of brave men from all walks of life, who have not asked what they could get out of our Nation but instead what they could give to it.

It is the history of a unique service — trained to fight on land and sea and now in the air as well.

Those of us who have had the privilege of serving in the Marine Corps value our experience as among the most precious of our lives. The fellowship of shared hardships and dangers in a worthy cause creates a close bond of comradeship. It is the basic reason for the cohesiveness of Marines and for the pride we have in the Corps and our loyalty to each other. Sometimes this takes the form of excessive boastfulness — a trait which naturally alienates others. But this is generally only the characteristic of the young and inexperienced. The older and the more mature are willing to let the record of the Corps speak for itself.

That is why this history is valuable. It tells the story of our service in brief outline without undue heroics. But Mr. Montross is not blind to our faults, and indeed confesses to a dereliction or two of which we were not previously aware.

In times past, the fact that the landing and use of Marines was not considered an act of war caused them to be employed on numerous occasions which were labeled "police actions" but which other peoples frequently termed "imperialism." In those cases, however, the Marines should not have been denounced, for they were the servants of policy and not its instigators. They served perhaps as forerunners of the international police force which the world will ultimately need to preserve the peace in retarded areas of the earth and to prevent small wars from expanding into larger ones.

This history by Lynn Montross tells the colorful story of these many interventions as well as the part which the Corps has played in the Mexican, Spanish-American and the two World Wars. Countries such as Haiti and Nicaragua come alive. Battles such as Château-Thierry, the Argonne, Guadalcanal, Tarawa, Saipan, Tinian, Peleliu, Iwo Jima, and Okinawa are rescued from forgetfulness and oblivion. In the Pacific, the Corps was almost invariably given the "hot" beaches and the heavily fortified islands to attack. Any grumbling over these assignments was minor compared with the deep pride we felt at being entrusted with the most difficult and dangerous tasks.

In all these engagements the Corps has never struck its colors and never flinched in battle. Its record should inspire the youth to similar deeds of valor and, we submit, should lead to a deeper understanding and appreciation on the part of the mature. The republic indeed needs such shock troops who reckon the worth of life neither in wealth accumulated nor in power exercised but rather in effort and sacrifice expended, and, if need be, in blood outpoured.

In war, the Marines have fought to defend our country. In peace, they have had to struggle to prevent the Corps from being abolished. For the planners of the general staff have worked either to eliminate the Corps or to relegate it to guard, ceremonial and longshore duties. Such was the celebrated Collins plan of 1946-47, which only Congress stopped. The theoretical logicians of the organization charts have generally agreed with these planners and have handed down their fiat that the Nation should not have two ground armies, and that the Marine Corps as such should disappear.

But as this history abundantly demonstrates, there is more to life than organization charts. Morale and fighting spirit are far more important. These qualities are better imbued by membership in a corps with the noble traditions of brave men than by service as a numbered unit in a huge undifferentiated mass army. For men need immediate loyalties which will undergird and reinforce those which are greater but which may seem to many to be too abstract and too far away to be all-compelling.

We all hope that the terrors of nuclear war may be avoided; as an alternative, the advantages of limited force which will do a minimum of damage to the structure of society are becoming more evident. The Marines cannot, of course, solve the great problems of war and peace or deal with the perplexing issues of international relations. But the Nation may breathe more easily because of their presence as faithful servants and, indeed, watchdogs of the republic. We hope that in return the people will not allow the Marines to be crushed out but rather will help the Corps to live on with the same heroism that has characterized its past.

Let us be proud as we scan the history of the Marine Corps and let us see to it that it is not banished from the service of our country.

PAUL H. DOUGLAS
U. S. Senator from Illinois
and Lt. Colonel, USMCR (Ret.)

CONTENTS

THE UNITED STATES MARINES

A Pictorial History

THE MARINES' HYMN

From the Halls of Montezuma
To the shores of Tripoli,
We fight our country's battles
In the air, on land and sea;
First to fight for right and freedom,
And to keep our honor clean,
We are proud to claim the title
Of United States Marine.

Our flag's unfurl'd to every breeze
From dawn to setting sun;
We have fought in every clime and place
Where we could take a gun;
In the snow of far-off Northern lands
And in sunny tropic scenes,
You will find us always on the job —
The United States Marines.

Here's health to you and to our Corps
Which we are proud to serve;
In many a strife we've fought for life
And never lost our nerve;
If the Army and the Navy
Ever gaze on Heaven's scenes,
They will find the streets are guarded
by United States Marines.

FIRST TO FIGHT

The Army has the land for its province, and the Navy claims the sea. The Air Force makes the sky its empire, and the Coast Guard is concerned with our own shores.

What, then, is left for the United States Marines?

This question is not as simple as it may seem. It has been earnestly debated by Congressmen and high-ranking staff officers for more than a century. Sometimes, indeed, the very existence of the Marine Corps has been at stake; efforts have been made to cut its appropriations on the grounds that it duplicated the functions of one of the other armed services.

For the answer is that the versatile Marines haven't confined their operations to any one element. Since 1775 the "soldiers of the sea" have fought as often in jungle or mountain terrain as on swaying decks. They have been jacks-of-all-trades, militarily speaking, and masters of a good many. They were among the pioneers in combat aviation, and they have specialized in a tactical

element of their own — the shot-swept beaches, representing the transition from ship to shore in an amphibious landing.

Still, the adverb "where" is not as important as "when" to Marines, who cherish these three words from their spirited hymn:

"First to fight . . ."

International usage has long sanctioned the tacit assumption that the Marines, as transitory shipborne forces, can land on foreign soil without the implication of hostilities usually associated with invading troops. And what was once a cabled report has been repeated so often in our history as to become a hackneyed expression:

"The Marines have landed and the situation is well in hand."

More than two hundred amphibious landings have been made during the eight generations of Marine Corps history. Some of them have been bloodless routine performances. But others, such as Tarawa and Iwo Jima, rank among the hardest-fought actions of American history.

1

Above, from left to right, are depicted a Marine sergeant of 1780, a sergeant of 1812 and a major of 1834.

From the War of 1812 to the Civil War, the clothing allowance was about $30 a year for enlisted men.

Eight Generations of Marines

During the first half of the present century there were only a few years when the Marines were not on active foreign duty somewhere. Mexico, China, the Philippines, Santo Domingo, Nicaragua — all these were occupied by Marines at a time when all the rest of their countrymen were at peace.

With such a tradition to uphold, the Marines have been called "America's Force in Readiness" — a highly trained body of fighting men instantly available for any national emergency. In World War I they fought as infantry in a Regular Army division. In World War II they were amphibious assault troops as well as jungle fighters. And in Korea they fought in the mountains, in the streets and on the beaches.

The intricacies of the close relationship between the Navy and the Marine Corps are sometimes puzzling. The chain of command varies from one operation to another, but the spirit of Navy-Marine relations was summed up by Secretary of the Navy Robert B. Anderson in 1953, when he referred to the Marine Corps as "the partner of the Navy."

"Together," he continued, "they have but one reason for being: to insure the freedom of the seas in peacetime, and insure their control and use on our side in time of war.

"They are in every sense of the word a team — an indispensable team to an America depend-ent absolutely on free use of the seas both in peace and war.

"Separate but inseparable, they have throughout their long association set an example of co-operation and mutual support unexcelled anywhere in the annals of military history."

In 1927 a directive of the Joint Board of the Army and Navy (forerunner of the Joint Chiefs of Staff) gave the Marine Corps the mission of "special preparation in the conduct of landing operations." This was the beginning of the Navy-Marine partnership in amphibious assault techniques which was seen at its best in World War II.

Another example of Navy-Marine co-operation may be found in the development of modern body armor from lightweight plastics. Hundreds of lives were saved during the Korean conflict by the Marine armored vest, weighing eight and a half pounds, which can stop a submachine-gun slug, a .45-caliber pistol bullet and most shell or grenade fragments.

There was a tactical as well as a humanitarian principle at stake; for if the vest could prevent half the serious wounds of this nature, it meant that 50 per cent of the enemy's best anti-personnel weapons had in effect been silenced! Field surveys indicated that this was not an unreasonable expectation, and both the Army and Marine Corps issued their own types of armored vests to all combat troops before the war ended.

FROM FLINTLOCKS
TO MACHINE GUNS

Marine uniforms from 1780 to 1945, as shown on these two pages, were painted by Lieutenant Colonel John H. Magruder III, USMCR, curator of the Marine Corps museums in Washington, D. C., and Quantico, Virginia.

From a strictly historical viewpoint, of course, it isn't likely that many Marine enlisted men of the American Revolution and War of 1812 were ever so smartly uniformed as these pictures indicate. Marines of 1776, like the soldiers and sailors of that day, probably wore the garments they had on their backs when taken into the service. Uniforms were received from France, but there were far from enough of them to go around.

There was, however, one article of Marine apparel used in the nation's first two wars which left a mark on history. That was the high leather stock worn by Marines of 1780 and 1812. It served a double purpose: it compelled the recruit to hold his head high, as befitted a Marine, and it didn't "show dirt." And though the stock itself is now a museum piece, the nickname "Leatherneck" has survived down to the present day.

At the right (upper to lower) are shown a sergeant of 1859 and a corporal of 1871. Below (left to right) are a sergeant of 1898, a corporal of 1918 and an island-hopping private of World War II.

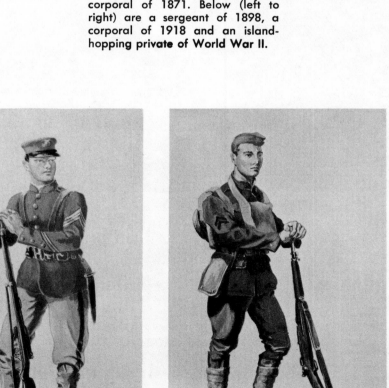

Our Flag's Unfurl'd to Every Breeze

These words from the Marines' Hymn may be taken at face value, for it is a cherished tradition that there are few places on this earth where Marines haven't served. In their capacity as legation guards, the men of the Corps have long been familiar with the capitals of Europe and Asia.

Less to be cherished is the fact that the reputation of the Marines for physical valor has outshone the important contributions they have made to the intellectual side of warfare in the twentieth century.

It has been said many times that the English-speaking peoples are never prepared at the outbreak of war. But there is at least one rule-proving exception. In spite of the humiliations suffered at Pearl Harbor, the United States possessed on that December day in 1941 what a

British military analyst has termed "in all probability the most far-reaching tactical innovation of the war."

This was the conclusion of Major General J. F. C. Fuller in his history of World War II. He was referring to the system of amphibious assault tactics worked out by the Marine Corps in partnership with the Navy during the 1930's. Never once did it sustain a major defeat in World War II while opening up Africa and Europe to invasion, as well as the Japanese-held islands of the Pacific.

Oran, Casablanca, Sicily, Tarawa, Kwajalein, Attu, Kiska, Peleliu, Saipan, Normandy, Iwo Jima, Okinawa — these were some of the victories won by American amphibious tactics. Four Army divisions were trained by the Marines in

A **Marine battle flag** of the Mexican War is shown on the opposite page and, above, a flag of 1898. Today's flags are carried ceremonially by color guards such as the one shown at right. Gone forever are the gallant days when a regiment carried its tattered flag into battle and men died to keep it flying.

ship-to-shore landing techniques, and the Army made valuable contributions of its own to a similar field of tactics, the shore-to-shore operation.

As a result of studies and tests held in cooperation with the Navy after World War II, the Marine Corps took the lead in developing the two foremost tactical innovations of the Korean conflict — the combat helicopter and modern body armor made of lightweight plastics. The first front-line helicopter operations of history were conducted by Marine squadrons using techniques adopted on the basis of prewar experiments. Command and staff flights, rescue missions, casualty evacuations, wire laying, frontline supply, troop transport — these were Marine operations which became commonplace only a few months after being announced in headlines.

We Have Fought in Every Clime and Place
Where We Could Take a Gun...

MARINE LANDINGS
IN TIME OF PEACE

On these pages are shown four of the spots where Marines have landed as trouble-shooters in time of peace. The bugler in the photograph on Page 6 is blowing reveille for the Marine brigade sent to Iceland in 1941. The machine-gun emplacement is manned by Marines of the regiment which landed in Shanghai to protect American interests during the civil war battles of 1927.

The Marine biplanes shown above are flying over an extinct volcano in Nicaragua during the U. S. intervention of the early 1930's. And at the right are Marines marching through the streets of Vladivostok in 1918, when the Whites and Reds were contending for power after the Revolution.

In the Air

The gull-winged Corsair! Never in the annals of American military aviation has there been a more rugged and effective fighter-bomber than this Chance-Vought aircraft. A veteran of two wars, World War II and the Korean conflict, the first F4Us were flown in February, 1943, by a Marine fighter squadron in the South Pacific. The Corsair was still going strong ten years later, even though it was being replaced by the Grumman Panther Jet.

The Marines liked to think of the Corsair as their own plane, since it was so strongly identified with the tactics of close air support. Pilots were given intensive infantry training, so as to inculcate firsthand knowledge of the problems of the ground forces. Thus the airmen were better enabled to support attacking Marine infantry with low-altitude strikes. At its best, Marine close air support was close indeed, the purpose being to pin down the enemy just ahead of the advancing Marine ground forces, which would be upon him before he had time to recover from the bombs, napalm (jellied gasoline), rockets and 20mm cannon or machine-gun fire poured into him by the snarling Corsairs.

Probably the first recorded instance of close air support directed from the ground took place during the Marine occupation of Nicaragua in 1927. Even in that day of the biplane, the Marines had a Corsair — the Chance-Vought 02U observation plane — which spotted a patrol besieged by the enemy in the jungle. The beleaguered infantrymen put out colored panels to direct the Marine pilots, who made a low-level bombing and strafing attack to extricate the patrol.

Air drops of supplies and air evacuation of casualties were also introduced by Marine pilots in Haiti and Nicaragua during the 1920's. Necessity was indeed the parent of tactical invention in these jungle operations, and the lessons were afterwards incorporated into tactical theory by the officers of the Marine Corps Schools at Quantico.

Although German fliers of 1940 were popularly credited with introducing dive-bombing, Marine pilots relied on that technique in the 1920's, when they put into effect the concept of "airborne artillery" in Haiti and Nicaragua. There was no other means of supporting patrols which operated in jungle terrain too primitive for pack howitzers, and the Corsairs were good ambush insurance.

9

On Land

The term "Horse Marines" has a comic opera flavor, yet the historical fact is that U. S. Marines have been trained and served as mounted troops whenever they found it expedient. Pictured above is a detachment in China during the Marine occupation of the 1920's, and on the opposite page is a mounted detachment in Haiti at about the same period. The Marines did not even scorn to rely upon donkeys in some of their operations in Caribbean islands.

The Marine bugler at the left was photographed in a sandbagged outpost of Alaska just before the outbreak of World War II. And at the top of Page 11 are shown some of the Marines who fought their way ashore at Vera Cruz, Mexico, in April, 1914. The seizure and imprisonment of American seamen was the "incident" which led President Wilson to order an intervention. Marines and Army troops remained at Vera Cruz eight months, while Mexico was in the throes of civil war. Meanwhile, Europe was plunged into World War I.

And on the Sea

Marines took a distinguished part in such sea battles of 1814 as the victory of the U. S. sloop *Wasp* over the British brig *Reindeer*. Artist John Clymer has shown two of the main missions of the Marine contingent: to serve as marksmen in the rigging and fighting tops, and to participate with pistol and cutlass in the attacks of boarding parties. In this particular action, the sailors and Marines gained the surrender of the enemy in an action lasting nineteen minutes.

On the opposite page are Marines on board an American battleship of 1912, when naval strength was computed in terms of armor plate and big guns. Another era of naval tactics is shown in the view of amphibious tractors landing Marines at Wonsan, Korea, in October, 1950.

Three different ages of sea warfare appear in these photographs, but sentry duty in harbor has changed but little. The sergeant on the left is finding it as lonesome a task as did the Marines of 1814.

In the Snow of Far-off Northern Lands
And in Sunny Tropic Scenes

You Will Find Us Always on the Job — The United States Marines

Sub-zero weather prevailed when the Marine tank on the opposite page was photographed in northeast Korea during the Chosin Reservoir breakout of December, 1950. Below, for contrast, is a photograph of a Marine encampment of 1912 at Guantanamo Bay, Cuba.

Mud and snow are piled up in front of the M-12 artillery sleds shown above on this page. They were photographed in Alaska during the spring of 1947, when a D-7 tractor was towing a 155mm howitzer. As for the sunny tropic scene, below is a column of marching Marines on Saipan soon after the amphibious victory of June, 1944.

At least the Marines are doing something about the weather these days. Special equipment for extremes of both heat and cold has added to troop efficiency, although, in the past, such trials were accepted as being inevitable.

In Many a Strife
We've Fought for Life

Three of the hardest fights of Marine history are shown on these pages. Above is an artist's conception of the victory of the USS *Constitution* over the British *Guerrière* in 1812, and on the opposite page is a painting of the storming of Chapultepec in the war with Mexico. The twentieth century is represented by a photograph of Marines attacking on the Meuse-Argonne front as World War I came to an end in the fall of 1918.

Although the Marines have given proof of their adaptability when it comes to tactical innovations, they cling to military doctrines which might be considered pessimistic, if not actually backward, by the more enthusiastic advocates of push-button warfare. The Marines believe that there is no comparatively easy and painless way of winning a war.

After World War II, this doctrine was considered old-fashioned by theorists, who held that an adversary could be strangled into submission if the flow of his vital military supplies was cut off by the long-distance pressure of strategic bombing.

The first great test came in Korea — a narrow peninsula so ridged with mountains that only a few roads and railways were available for the funneling of supplies from Manchuria. Here, surely, was a happy hunting ground for the bombing planes of a nation in complete control of the air over Korea! Yet the Chinese Reds were able to nourish two large-scale offensives, each involving several hundred thousand troops, during a six-week period in the winter of 1950-1951.

Some grievous losses, as well as bright victories, have fallen to the lot of the Marines. There was no more humiliating reverse than the rout of 1814, known derisively as the "Bladensburg Races." On the outskirts of Washington, a small army of militiamen ran from the redcoats, leaving the new capital a prey to the torch. The brave stand made by a handful of bluejackets and Marines is depicted by a Marine artist, Colonel Donald M. Dickson. Below is a photograph of a Marine patrol on Santo Domingo in 1917, when ambush was a constant peril. More Marines served on Caribbean islands during World War I than in France. These islands were our strategic shield, and President Wilson invoked an interpretation of the Monroe Doctrine when their security was imperiled by revolt and disorders.

And to Keep Our Honor Clean

The "day of infamy" at Pearl Harbor dates the photograph above, with the capsized USS *Oklahoma* and burning USS *Maryland* shown in the foreground. Below is a photograph of a wounded Marine being carried past a dead Japanese soldier on Iwo Jima. Marine casualties exceeded Federal Army losses at Gettysburg.

Proud to Serve

The United States Marines has long been the only branch of the armed service to issue enlisted men a dress uniform reminiscent of the days when warriors of all nations wore swaggering plumage. Well known in Bangkok, Teheran and other remote capitals is the familiar uniform of blue and gold, with a bold red stripe down the trousers.

No doubt it is pride in the uniform which explains the fondness of the Marines for parades and ceremonials, such as the color guard shown at the left and (below) the parade of Marine infantry and mounted troops photographed at Shanghai, China, in 1927.

Insistence on "spit and polish" has always been a tradition of a rough-and-ready corps, and Marines make every effort to add brilliance to an already blinding shoeshine. An Australian brand of shoe polish, discovered during World War II, found itself in possession of an unexpectedly large overseas market on the strength of Marine approval. Dry cleaners and pressers have always found Marine enlisted men the most constant of patrons.

About one hundred officers and nine thousand enlisted men make up this living emblem of the Marine Corps, photographed from the air, at the Marine Barracks, Parris Island, S. C., in 1919.

MARINES TO GUARD HEAVEN'S STREETS?

The last four lines of the Marines' Hymn express some doubt about the Army or Navy ever gazing upon Heaven's scenes, but leave no question about the Marines. An exponent of this spirit is Marine Sergeant Michael Fitzgerald (below), photographed while on recruiting duty in New York in 1916. The bulldog is "Sergeant Jiggs," whose enlistments papers were signed by Brigadier General Smedley Butler in 1922. Marines have seldom been famed for humility, but for unabashed cockiness it would be hard to beat the unidentified private first class on the opposite page, shown while serving with the United States Legation Guard at Peking, China, during the Japanese invasion of the 1930's. To be known as "an old China hand" was the peak of every Marine's ambition.

The Old Tun Tavern, Philadelphia

MARINES IN COCKED HATS

Night after night during the autumn of 1775, a window of the Tun Tavern gleamed bravely with candlelight after the rest of the Philadelphia waterfront was dark. In an upstairs room, seven gentlemen in knee breeches and silk stockings were gathered about a long table. The Maritime Committee of the Continental Congress was in session, and the members looked forward to a social glass of Madeira after finishing their business.

At the head of the table sat the chairman, John Adams of Massachusetts, who had made maritime affairs his foremost interest in the Continental Congress. The other members of the committee were Silas Deane of Connecticut, John Langdon of New Hampshire, Christopher Gadsden of South Carolina, Joseph Hewes of North

Carolina, Richard Henry Lee of Virginia, and Stephen Hopkins of Rhode Island.

As delegates to the Continental Congress, these men sat all day at the old State House, known today as Independence Hall. They had rented the room at the Tun Tavern so that their Maritime Committee sessions could be held in privacy until late hours of the night.

In the autumn of 1775, the leaders of American revolt still cherished British institutions, even though their political grievances had led them to defy George III and Parliament. The gentlemen of the Maritime Committee frankly made the naval institutions of the mother country their model. Thus the British Royal Marines, founded in 1664, were the inspiration for the resolution which brought into being the Continental Marines.

24

The historical resolution as it appeared in the Journals of the Continental Congress.

In the Beginning...

The historical resolution as it appeared in the Journals of the Continental Congress is shown above. Following are the few words which brought into being the Continental Marines on November 10, 1775:

"Resolved, that two Battalions of Marines be raised consisting of one Colonel two lieutenant Colonels, two Majors & Officers as usual in other regiments. That they consist of an equal number of privates with other battalions. That particular care be taken that no person be appointed to office or enlisted into said Battalions, but such as are good seamen, or so acquainted with maritime affairs as to be able to serve to advantage by sea, when required. That they be enlisted and commissioned to serve for and during the present war between Great Britain and the Colonies, unless dismissed by order of Congress. That they be distinguished by the names of the first and second battalions of American Marines, and that they be considered a part of the number, which the Continental Army before Boston is ordered to consist of."

Tun Tavern Meetings Long Cherished

Our forefathers, as rebels, may have been putting their heads into a noose, but they did not pull a long face. John Adams was to cherish, all the rest of his long life, the fondest recollections of the convivial meetings at the Tun Tavern in which the Marine resolution was discussed. Stephen Hopkins, who was patriarch of the Maritime Committee at the age of 70 and former governor of Rhode Island, was the most lively conversationalist in the group.

"Upon business, his experience and judgment were very useful," recalled Adams many years later. "But when the business of the day was over, he kept us in conversation till eleven and sometimes twelve o'clock. His custom was to drink nothing all day, nor till eight o'clock in the evening, and then his beverage was Jamaica spirit and water. It gave him wit, humor, anecdotes, science and learning. He had read Greek, Roman and British history, and was familiar with English poetry, particularly Pope, Thomson and Milton, and the flow of his soul made all his reading our own, and seemed to bring to recollection in all of us, all we had ever read."

In this urbane atmosphere, the Marine Corps had its beginnings. It is fitting, therefore, that the birthday should have been celebrated by Marines ever since with banquets, balls and cake-cutting ceremonies.

It is further appropriate that the officer recognized as founding father should have been a Philadelphia innkeeper, Samuel Nicholas. The oldest existing Marine commission, dated November 28, 1775, was made out to the 31-year-old captain, who would soon distinguish himself in the war's first amphibious combat landing.

The portrait is of Samuel Nicholas, recognized as the founding father of the Marine Corps, and the tablet marks the site of the old Tun Tavern on the Philadelphia waterfront. On Page 27 is a payroll of Captain Robert Mullan's Marine company in 1776, when pounds and shillings were still the currency.

1776 — Day Roll of Capt. Robert Mullan's

No	Men's Names		Date of Enlistmt	Mo. Days	£ s d
✓ 1	Robt. Mullan	Capt.	June 25th	5 . 6	
2	David Love	1st Lieut.	do. do.	5 . 6	
✓ 3	Hugh Montgomery	2 Lieut.	do. do.	5 . 6	
✓ 4	James Coakley	Serjt.	July 1st	5 . —	
✗ 5	Andrew Read	do.	Augt. 22d	3 . 9	£ 3 . 10 . 0
✗ 6	John McKinley	do. do.	2d	3 . 29	. . 6 . 0 . —
7	Warwick Hallabough	do.	Sept. 13th	2 . 10	. . 2 . 6 . —
✓ 8	George Murray	Corpl.	Aug. 27th	3 . 4	. . 3 . 2 . 4
✗ 9	Adam McFerson	do.	Octr. 22d	1 . 9	. . 1 . 1 . 6
✓ 10	John Cribs	do. do.	13th	1 . 10	. . 1 . 13 . —
✓ 11	Joseph Greenley	do.	Sept. 17th	2 . 14	. . 6 . 15 . 8
✗ 12	Collin York	Drumr.	June 25th	5 . 6	. . 0 . 16 . —
✗ 13	Peter York	Fifer	do. do.	5 . 6	. . 0 . 16 . —
✗ 14	John Hogg	Private	Aug. 21st	3 . 10	. . 3 . 6 . 0
✓ 15	William Barnett	do.	Sept. 1st	3 . —	. . 2 . 10 . —
✓ 16	Lawrence Lepee	do.	do. 3d	2 . 20	. . 2 . 6 . 0
✗ 17	Benjamin Wooden	do.	Aug. 12th	3 . 19	. . 4 . 11 . 8
✓ 18	Robt. Gilmore	do. do.	20th	3 . 3	. . 2 . 15 . —
✗ 19	William Allison	do.	Sept. 2d	2 . 29	. . 2 . 8 . 4
✗ 20	John Stone	do. do. do.		2 . 29	. . 2 . 8 . 4
21	Danl. Forrman	do. do. do.		2 . 29	. . 2 . 8 . 4
✓ 22	William Carcill	do.	Augt. 19th	3 . 12	. . 3 . 10 . —
✓ 23	Henry Sharp	do.	Sept. 1st	3 . —	. . 2 . 10 . —
✗ 24	George Campbell	do.	Augt. 4th	3 . 27	. . 4 . 15 . —
✓ 25	James McIllear	do. do.	8th	3 . 23	. . 4 . 8 . 4
✗ 26	Stephen Rutledge	do. do.	22d	3 . 9	. . 3 . 5 . —
✗ 27	James Stevenson	do. do. do.		3 . 9	. . 3 . 5 . —
28	Noter Gawden	do.	Sept. 9th	2 . 22	. . 1 . 16 . 0
✓ 29	Thomas Murphy	do. do.	2d	2 . 29	. . 2 . 8 . 4
✗ 30	Robt. Work	do.	Augt. 16th	3 . 15	. . 3 . 15 . —
31	Patrick Quigley	do.	July 16th	4 . 15	. . 7 . 5 . —
✓ 32	Mark Sullivan	do.	Sept. 10th	2 . 21	. . 1 . 15 . —
✓ 33	John McFall	do.	Augt. 5th	3 . 26	. . 4 . 13 . 4
✗ 34	William Stone	do.	Sept. 5th	2 . 26	. . 2 . 3 . 4
✗ 35	Stephen Archer	do.	Augt. 13th	3 . 18	. . 4 . 0 . —
✗ 36	James Cane	do.	Sept. 9th	2 . 22	. . 1 . 16 . 0
37	Danl. McCarty turnd over to Adora		Aug. 10th	3 . 21	
✗ 38	Michl. Kelly	do.	Sept. 12th	2 . 19	. . 1 . 11 . 0
39	Neil Farron	do.	Augt. 16th	3 . 15	. . 3 . 15 . —
✗ 40	William Beaucham	do.	Sept. 4th	2 . 27	. . 2 . 5 . —

In CONGRESS.

The DELEGATES of the UNITED STATES of New-Hampfhire, Maffachufetts-Bay, Rhode-Ifland, Connecticut, New-York, New-Jerfey, Pennfylvania, Delaware, Maryland, Virginia, North Carolina, South-Carolina, and Georgia, TO *Mr William Waterman*

WE, repofing efpecial Truft and Confidence in your Patriotifm, Valour, Conduct and Fidelity, DO, by thefe Prefents, conftitute and appoint you to be *firft Lieutenant of marines* in the Navy of the United States of North-America, fitted out for the defence of American Liberty, and for repelling every hoftile Invafion thereof. You are therefore carefully and diligently to difcharge the duty of *firft Lieutenant of marines* by doing and performing all manner of things thereunto belonging. And we do ftrictly charge and require all Officers, Marines and Seamen under your Command, to be obedient to your Orders as *firft Lieutenant of marines* And you are to obferve and follow fuch Orders and Directions from Time to Time, as you fhall receive from this or a future Congrefs of the United States, or Committee of Congrefs for that purpofe appointed, or Commander in Chief for the Time being of the Navy of the United States, or any other your fuperior Officer, according to the Rules and Difcipline of War, the Ufage of the Sea, and the Inftructions herewith given you, in Purfuance of the Truft repofed in you. This Commiffion to continue in Force until revoked by this or a future Congrefs. DATED at *Bofton April 29th 1778*

By Order of the CON

ATTEST. *Cha Thomfon fecy*   *Henry Laurens*, PRESIDENT.

This Marine commission, dated April 28, 1778, is signed by Henry Laurens and Charles Thomson, president and secretary, respectively, of the Continental Congress. It is made out to First Lieutenant William Waterman, who, as a captain in 1782, was the last Marine officer of the war mentioned in official records.

To Cut a Dash on Shore with His Girl and His Glass...

Recruiting posters have never been renowned for sober veracity, and American young men in 1775 were promised a daily "Pound of BEEF or PORK, — One Pound of BREAD, — Flour, Raisins, Butter, Cheese, Oatmeal . . . Tea, Sugar, &c. &c. And a Pint of the best WINE, or Half a Pint of the best RUM or BRANDY; together with a Pint of LEMONADE." But it is not likely that such noble rations materialized for Continental Marines, destined to subsist on flinty salt pork and biscuit while at sea.

The Tun Tavern remained in the Marine scheme of things when its proprietor, Robert Mullan, was given a commission as captain. And his hostelry became the headquarters for Marine recruiting.

Captain Mullan's appeal was in the best tradition of the recruiting poster when he asked rhetorically where a young man of 1775 could find "such a fair opportunity of reaping Glory and Riches, as in the Continental Marines, a Corps daily acquiring new Honors. . . . once em-

barked in [the] American Fleet, he finds himself in the midst of Honor and Glory, surrounded by a set of fine Fellow[s], Strangers to Fear, and who strike Terror through the Hearts of their Enemies wherever they go!"

If this inducement fell short, the single man was further assured that in port he would be "enabled to cut a Dash on shore with his GIRL and his GLASS, that might be envied by a Nobleman, — Take courage, then, seize the Fortune that awaits you, repair to the MARINE RENDEZVOUS, where in a FLOWING BOWL OF PUNCH . . . you shall drink **Long Live The United States, and Success to the Marines."**

The Tun Tavern seems to have been virtually the administrative headquarters of the Continental Marines. But it proved easier at first to find patriotic and adventurous young men than arms and equipment. The Pennsylvania Committee of Safety came to the rescue with donations of muskets and gunpowder, but the Continental Marines continued to be handicapped by shortages.

GREAT ENCOURAGEMENT

AMERICAN REVOLUTION

What a Brilliant Prospect does this Event hold out to every Lad of Spirit, who is inclined to try his Fortune in that highly renowned Corps

The Continental Marines

When every Thing that swims the Seas must be a

PRIZE!

Thousands are at this moment endeavoring to get on Board Privateers, where they serve without Pay or Reward of any kind whatsoever, so certain does their Chance appear of enriching themselves by PRIZE MONEY! What an enviable Station then must the *CONTINENTAL MARINE* hold,—who with far superior Advantages to thefe, has the additional benefit of liberal Pay, and plenty of the best Provisions, with a good and well appointed Ship under him, the Pride and Glory of the Continental Navy; furely every Man of Spirit muft blufh to remain at Home in Inactivity and Indolence, when his Country needs his Assistance.

Where then can he have fuch a fair opportunity of reaping Glory and Riches, as in the Continental Marines, a Corps daily acquiring new Honors, and here, when once embarked in American Fleet, he finds himself in the midft of Honor and Glory, furounded by a fet of fine fellow, Strangers to Fear, and who ftrike Terror through the Hearts of their Enemies wherever they go!

He has likewise the infpiring idea to know, that while he fcour the Ocean to protect the Liberty of these states, that the Hearts and good Wifhes of the whole American people attend him, pray for his fuccefs, and participate in his Glory!! Lofe no Time then, my Fine Fellows, in embracing the glorious Opportunity that awaits you; YOU WILL RECEIVE

Seventeen Dollars Bounty,

And on your Arrival at Head Quarters, be comfortably and genteely CLOTHED.—And fpirited young BOYS of a promifing Appearance, who are Five Feet Six Inches high, WILL RECEIVE TEN DOLLARS, and equal Advantages of PROVISIONS and CLOTHING with the Men. And thofe who wish only to enlist for a limited Service, fhall receive a Bounty of SEVEN DOLLARS, and Boys FIVE. In Fact, the Advantages which the MARINE poffefes, are too numerous to mention here, but among the many, it may not be amifs to state.—*That if he has a WIFE or aged PARENT, he can make them an Allotment of half his PAY; which will be regularly paid without any Trouble to them, or to whomsoever he may directs that being well Clothed and Fed on Board Ship, the Remainder of his PAY and PRIZE MONEY will be clear in Reserve for the Relief of his Family or his own private Purposes. The Single Young Man on his Return to Port, finds himself enabled to cut a Dafh on Shore with his GIRL and his GLASS, that might be envied by a Nobleman.—Take Courage then, seize the Fortune that awaits you, repair to the MARINE RENDEZVOUS, where in a FLOWING BOWL of PUNCH, an Three Times Three, you shall drink*

Long Live The United States, and Success to the Marines.

The Daily Allowance of a Marine when embarked, is—One Pound of BEEF or PORK,—One Pound of BREAD,—Flour, Raisins, Butter, Cheese, Oatmeal, Molasses, Tea, Sugar, &c. &c. And a Pint of the beft WINE, or Half a Pint of the best RUM or BRANDY; together with a Pint of LEMONADE. They have liberty in warm Countries, a plentiful Allowance of the choicest FRUIT. And what can be more handsome than the Marines Proportion of PRIZE MONEY, when a Sergeant shares equal with the First Class of Petty Officers, such as Midshipmen, Assistant Surgeons, &c. which is Five Shares each; a Corporal with the Second Class, which is Three Shares each; and the Private with the Able Seamen, one Share and a Half each.

Desiring greater Particulars, and a more full Account of the many Advantages of this invaluable Corps, apply to CAPTAIN MULLAN, at TUN TAVERN, where the Bringer of a Recruit will receive THREE DOLLARS.

January, 1776

Marine Recruiting Poster of January, 1776

First of the Marine Landings

Captain Samuel Nicholas and his Marines did their best to save the recruiting posters from hyperbole by covering themselves with glory in the little Continental Navy's first offensive operation. Commodore Esek Hopkins and his squadron of eight small warships had as their objective the British island of New Providence in the Bahamas, where it was hoped to seize desperately needed military supplies.

About 220 Marines and 50 bluejackets stormed ashore on March 3, 1776, under cover of gunfire from the American sloop *Providence* and the schooner *Wasp*. No harm came to the attackers from several round shot, fired by the cannon of Fort Montague before it capitulated. Nicholas then managed to convince the defenders of the main stronghold, Fort Nassau, that resistance was futile.

The persuasive Marine captain gained a surrender without firing a shot or suffering a single casualty, though the 71 captured cannon included 40 loaded for his reception. This bloodless victory enabled the Americans to take large military stores to Philadelphia.

Marines also fought as infantry in some of the land battles of the American Revolution. As commanding officer of the Continental Marines, with the rank of major, Nicholas led a battalion attached to the little army of Colonel John Cadwalader in December, 1776. General George Washington was encamped on the Pennsylvania shore of the Delaware, after completing a disastrous retreat across New Jersey in which his army had dwindled to fewer than 5,000 effectives.

In spite of his weakness, the commander in chief was planning to strike by surprise on Christmas night at the Hessian outpost in the village of Trenton. Cadwalader's division was to cross the

Captain Nicholas's Marines probably did not cut as dashing a figure as those shown in an artist's conception of the New Providence landing, but they captured supplies of great value to their cause. On the opposite page is an artist's idea of the legendary occasion when General Washington commended Marine Captain Andrew Porter for his bravery at the second battle of Trenton, January 2, 1777.

river at Burlington, but he was unable to land his artillery and returned to the Pennsylvania side.

Nicholas and his Marines did not participate in Washington's famous victory, but a few days later they crossed the river and joined him at Trenton. And on January 2, 1777, after Cornwallis arrived by forced marches, the Marines gave a good account of themselves in the second battle of Trenton. Nicholas and his men also took part in the battle of Princeton the next day, and accompanied the commander in chief when he went into winter quarters at Morristown, New Jersey. This brilliant little two-week campaign was the moral turning point of the American Revolution.

In the autumn of 1777, the Continental Marines had a hand in the American attempt to blockade the Delaware River and prevent waterborne supplies from reaching General Sir William Howe's British army occupying Philadelphia. German mercenaries met a bloody repulse while trying to storm Fort Mercer, the American stronghold on the New Jersey shore. But a new channel was created by the heavy timbers with pointed iron stakes which the Americans had sunk as a barrier to the British fleet. And the blockade failed after the warships obliterated Fort Mifflin, on the Pennsylvania side, with a terrific bombardment which sent a thousand shot and shell screaming into the works every twenty minutes.

Dickson

The Continental Navy couldn't hope to challenge wave-ruling Britannia during the American Revolution, but John Paul Jones set a deathless tradition of heroism for his adopted country on the moonlight night of September 23, 1779, when his *Bon Homme Richard* defeated and captured the British *Serapis*. This scene in the fighting top of Jones's ship was painted by a present-day Marine artist, Colonel Donald W. Dickson. It was the perilous duty of the Marines to pick off opponents with musket fire, but meanwhile they made such good targets that 67 of the *Richard's* Marines were killed or wounded. The ship, a converted merchantman, was so riddled by British fire that she had to be abandoned. Jones and his crew sailed the *Serapis* to Holland.

MARINES TAKE PART IN TWO LOSING FIGHTS

Continental Marines were represented on all the crews of American warships during the Revolution. They also had a hand in most of the river and harbor operations, including the blockade of the Delaware River just below Philadelphia in October and November, 1777. A contemporary water color (below), done by a British officer and published in London about 1779, shows Admiral Lord Richard Howe's British fleet bombarding Fort Mifflin on Mud Island, near the mouth of the Schuylkill River. The fire of the warships was supplemented by the cannonading of shore batteries, and after a terrific pounding the Americans evacuated a fort reduced to rubble. This meant an end to the blockade and the opening of the Delaware to ships supplying the British army in Philadelphia.

Another contemporary water color (right) shows the British ships in Penobscot Bay, Maine, during the disastrous American amphibious operation in the summer of 1779. About 150 Marines landed and seized Nautilus Island, commanding the anchorage of the British squadron, but prospects of victory were frittered away by quarreling and indecisive Massachusetts leaders, among whom was Paul Revere.

Thus the principal amphibious operation of the American Revolution ended in a defeat for the attackers, as a consequence of their own mistakes.

At a Regimental Court Martial held
at Philada Barracks on the 24th Novr 1776
Ordered by Major Saml Nicholas Esqr.
Capt Robt Mullan President

Leut James McClure } Members { Leut Wm Gillmore
Leut Abel Morgan   Leut Hugh Montgomery

Henry Hasson a Private in Capt Robt Mullan's
Company of Marines, Confind for Desertion
and for Quiting his Guard ———
on being Askt whether he was Guilty of
the Charge or not. he Plead Guilty of Both
therefore the Court Sentence him to have
Fifty Lashes for Desertion & Twenty one
Lashes for Quiting his Guard without

Deserter Given 71 Lashes

Americans fighting for their liberties did not think it inconsistent for flogging to be a military punishment. As this record of a Marine court-martial shows, Private Henry Hasson of Major Nicholas's battalion was sentenced "to have fifty Lashes for Desertion & Twenty one Lashes for quiting his Guard without leave of his Officers, on his bare back well laid on at the head of his Company."

Although such punishments would seem barbarous today, culprits endured them with stoicism in 1776, and they bit on a bullet in order to bear the pain. It is noteworthy, moreover, that Private Hasson might have fared worse in the Marine Corps of today for such serious offenses in time of war as desertion and abandoning his post without leave while on guard duty.

Sentences of 500 lashes were not unknown in the British Army during the late eighteenth century. An American wagoner was sentenced to this punishment, in the French and Indian War, for knocking a British officer down. But Dan Morgan must have been endowed with a hearty sense of humor, for he chuckled all the rest of his life when he recalled that the British count fell one lash short. And on the fields of Saratoga and Cowpens, during the American Revolution, he got his revenge.

THE IDEAL
AND THE REAL

The Revolution was a poor man's war, and the difference between the real and the ideal in Marine uniforms is depicted by artist H. C. McBarron, Jr. The two enlisted men are wearing the handsome but seldom used green and red uniform of the Continental Marines. A more common sight was the nondescript attire of the hastily raised Marines of Benedict Arnold's fleet on Lake Champlain. These volunteers were country lads from New England who wore their garments of everyday life, embellished with such military touches as they could contrive. But Arnold's Marines put up a good fight in the lake battle of Valcour Island. And even though the outweighed American squadron was destroyed, it delayed the British for so long that the invading army had to return to its Canadian base. It was probably Arnold's greatest contribution during the war to the cause that he was later to betray.

A **painting** on an old pitcher shows the ship *Industry* of Boston, Captain Gamaliel Bradford, engaging four French privateers on July 8, 1800. They were driven off after a hot action of ninety minutes.

Marine Corps Revived in 1798

After winning independence in the American Revolution, the United States set a precedent for the future by promptly disbanding nearly all the armed forces that had won the victory. Fewer than a hundred soldiers of the Continental Army were retained as guards, and the Continental Navy and Marines simply ceased to exist.

Unfortunately, the troubled era of the French Revolution was not an ideal period in which to depend for security on the good will of other countries. And when both the French privateers and the Barbary corsairs began preying upon American shipping, Congress hastily revived the Navy and Marine Corps.

It is not merely a coincidence that these acts were passed during the administration of John Adams, who has every right to be known as "father of the United States Navy." On the day after signing the act restoring the Marine Corps, the President appointed Major William Ward Burrows as the commandant. The act of July 11,

1798, provided for 1 major, 4 captains, 16 first lieutenants, 12 second lieutenants, 96 noncommissioned officers, 32 fifes and drums, and 720 privates. New warships were rapidly being put into commission, and early in the summer of 1798, the young republic entered into an undeclared naval war with the France of the corrupt Directory.

"Millions for defense but not one cent for tribute!" was the American slogan as preparations were made for a major war on land as well as sea. America's two most famous warships of the Age of Sail were launched in time to win their first victories. The *Constellation*, with 41 Marines attached, captured the 40-gun French *Insurgente* and defeated the 52-gun *Vengeance*. The *Constitution*, carrying a detachment of 50 Marines under Captain Daniel Carmick, took three French prizes. But the most active ship of all was the little *Enterprise*, with 16 Marines on board. During the year 1800 alone, this brig captured nine

French privateers and recaptured eleven American vessels.

More than eighty ships flying the tricolor were sunk or captured before France came to terms. But there was to be no peace on the sea, for the expeditions against the Barbary states were to follow.

Even though the interlude was brief, it proved to be long enough for the hurried beating of swords into plowshares which is the postscript to every American war. The undeclared war with France had scarcely ended before Congress passed the Peace Establishment Act, providing for a drastic reduction in armed forces. The sale of all naval vessels except the thirteen largest warships was authorized, and only six of them were to be kept in commission, with skeleton crews. Each of the thirteen vessels was assigned a guard of eight Marines, in addition to a few sailors.

President Jefferson continued the policy of retrenchment on May 11, 1802, when he ordered all Marines at navy yards discharged, with the exception of a sergeant, a corporal and 15 privates at Boston, New York, Philadelphia, Washington and Norfolk. Reductions were also made in the number of Marine artisans and mechanics.

These cuts resulted in a Marine Corps numbering only 23 officers and 483 enlisted men in February, 1803. And it was the following year that the naval operations against the Barbary corsairs reached a climax.

One of the first American victories in the undeclared naval war with France was won by the 20-gun *Delaware*, a converted packet, when she fought and captured the French ship *La Croyable* in an action of 1798.

"Old Ironsides" Is Still Afloat

This photograph of the USS *Constitution* was taken in New York Harbor, with steamships in the background, during the old ship's triumphal voyage of the early 1930's, after her fourth and last restoration. The greater part of the $650,000 raised for this purpose was composed of the donations of school children.

Launched at Boston in 1797, the *Constitution* was originally built of seasoned live oak and red cedar. She was given the nickname of "Old Ironsides" during her famous victory over the *Guerrière,* when British roundshot bounced off a hull armored with 21½ inches of oak.

In this battle the American frigate carried 55 guns and a crew of 456 men. Following are her dimensions: length over all, 204 feet; beam, 44 feet, 8 inches; draft 22 feet, 6 inches; gun range 1,200 yards.

Constellation to Be Restored

In the late 1950's it appeared that the historic old frigate *Constellation* might be doomed to oblivion as the consequence of neglect. Launched in 1797, a few weeks before the *Constitution* took to the sea, the *Constellation* never seemed to appeal as much to the popular imagination. The old relic was deteriorating to the point where restoration would have been virtually impossible when a group of patriotic Baltimore citizens arranged to have her towed to her original home port from Boston. After reconstruction along her original lines, the old frigate will be on permanent exhibit at Baltimore.

In 1902, when this photograph was taken, the *Constellation* was rounding out a long and useful career as naval training ship at Newport, R. I. She had served in the same capacity at the United States Naval Academy, Annapolis, Md.

Above is a view of O'Bannon's Marines on the march, as imagined by an artist. Several insurrections took place and on several occasions Christians and Moslems came near to battle along the way.

Camel Marines March 600 Miles

The war with the Barbary States was a naval conflict, yet the most remarkable Marine exploit was a 600-mile march from Alexandria, Egypt, to Derne (Derna), Tripoli. The inception was an American attempt to place a more friendly ruler on the throne of Tripoli.

William Eaton, a former U. S. Army officer, was selected as agent of a cloak-and-dagger plot which had official backing. On March 8, 1805, he set out across the Libyan desert with Hamet, pretender to the throne, and 90 of his followers, reinforced at the last moment by 38 Greeks and a party of Arabian horsemen. Eaton's only dependable men, however, were the seven U.S. Marines, headed by Lieutenant Presley N. O'Bannon.

American warships supplied the column along the coastal route and supported O'Bannon with naval gunfire on April 25, 1805, when he led the assault on Derne, which was defended by a garrison of 800 men. Understandably, the first effort failed. But the Marine leader won a foothold in a second attack, and the defenders fled when he turned their own cannon against them. The inhabitants promptly declared for Hamet, but he was unable to make himself ruler of Tripoli, and peace negotiations between his country and the United States led to an evacuation of Derne.

Inscriptions in both English and Arabic are shown on the plaque marking the site of the fort stormed by Presley O'Bannon and his Marines. The ruins were a landmark during the desert campaigns of World War II.

This portrait of Presley O'Bannon was taken from an old miniature.

A snapshot of 1956 shows the ruins of the fort at Derne (Derna), Tripoli, where the Stars and Stripes flew for the first time in the Old World. The site is known to the present day as "the American fort."

Above is a painting of a hand-to-hand fight, on the deck of an Algerine frigate, in which Stephen Decatur led a boarding party of U. S. bluejackets and Marines. The corsairs were no match for the Americans in this kind of fighting, as Decatur demonstrated more than once.

This bombardment of Tripoli by the *Constitution* (left) took place on August 4, 1804. It was one of five cannonades which persuaded the rulers of that Barbary state to abandon attempts to collect tribute for promises not to prey upon American shipping in the Mediterranean Sea.

Major William W. Burrows was commandant of the Marine Corps from 1798 to 1804, during the period of the naval expeditions against the Barbary corsairs. Almost the entire naval strength of the young republic was operating in the Mediterranean by 1804, and 400 Marine officers and men were carried on the warships, which compelled Algiers and Tunis as well as Tripoli to come to terms. This put an end to the raids on American seaborne commerce until a decade later, when the pirates violated their treaties.

Sacketts Harbour on Lake Ontaro.

Sackett's Harbor (above), on Lake Ontario, was the scene of a British amphibious assault in May, 1813. U. S. garrison forces, including Marines, repulsed the redcoats and drove them back to their warships.

Lake battles were a unique feature of early American wars. The contemporary painting (below) shows Oliver Hazard Perry's famous victory over a British squadron of six ships in the battle of Lake Erie.

Perry's Victory on Lake Erie.

Marines had a prominent part in the victory of the American 18-gun sloop-of-war *Wasp* over the British 18-gun brig *Frolic,* as shown in the painting on the left. The two evenly matched vessels fought for 43 minutes in heavy seas on October 17, 1812. Only 20 men of the British crew of 110 were left unhurt when the *Wasp's* Marines led a boarding party and took possession of the enemy ship.

Sea battles were a much cherished theme of nineteenth-century artists, and the fights with the Barbary corsairs provided inspiring material, as did the ship duels of the War of 1812. Below is another painting (see also Page 42) of the USS *Constitution* sailing boldly into the harbor of the city of Tripoli, followed by six American gunboats, and bombarding enemy shore batteries and gunboats. During the first six months of the War of 1812, the little U. S. Navy captured five British warships. One of these occasions, the surrender of the British sloop-of-war *Alert,* 20 guns, to the American 32-gun frigate *Essex,* is shown in the painting on the right. Considering the American advantage, the outcome was not a great triumph. Although the Americans made an excellent showing in single combat, British sea power soon overwhelmed them.

The portrait is of Lieutenant Colonel Franklin Wharton, commandant of the Marine Corps from 1804 to 1820. He was among the officials who departed from Washington just ahead of the redcoats on August 23, 1814, after the rout of American militiamen at Bladensburg. The Marine commandant's quarters, depicted in the artist's sketch on Page 47, was the only public building to escape the flames when the British burned the city.

The "mansion" at Eighth and Eye Streets, S. E., as shown in a recent photograph, is now the most venerable building of a capital which was scarcely more than a village in 1814. Marine commandants have made it their official residence ever since Colonel Wharton's rude eviction. Some of the oldest and most cherished traditions of the Marine Corps are associated with this famous old landmark.

FROM THE MUD TO THE STARS

The War of 1812 was a period of violent contrasts for Americans, whose victories were tarnished by some of the most disgraceful defeats in the nation's history. One of the brighter episodes is recalled on the opposite page by a photograph of the Marine detachment's morning report in Oliver Hazard Perry's fleet, the summer before his celebrated triumph. Below it is a painting of the duel between the USS frigate *United States,* commanded by Stephen Decatur, and HMS *Macedonian.* On October 25, 1812, the British frigate's masts and rigging were shot away in less than an hour and she was compelled to surrender.

Fights between British and American ships were conducted with such spirit that the loser was usually a wreck. It was deemed a disgrace for a ship to give up before she was helpless.

The battle of New Orleans on January 8, 1815, as depicted by an artist, is memorable for the fact that the treaty of peace had been signed in London two weeks before. The news did not reach this country in time to save the invaders from one of the most crushing defeats suffered by British arms since Bannockburn. Major Daniel Carmick, whose portrait is shcwn above, led the Marine contingent fighting with General Andrew Jackson's motley army, but died later from the effects of a wound inflicted by a rocket. The American victory did much to wipe out the disgrace of such reverses as the rout at Bladensburg.

MORING REPORT of a Detachment of Marines on board

the U. States' Brig.   Oliver H. Perry, Esq. Commanding.

SITUATION.	Sergeants.	Corporals.	Music.	Privates.	Total.	REMARKS.
Present fit for duty,	2	2	"	22	26	
Sick, - -	"	"	"	2	2	In Hospital, 1.
On command, -	"	1	3	"	4	
Confined, -	"	"	"	1	1	Desertion.
On furlough, -	"	"	"	"	"	
Absent without leave,	"	"	"	"	"	
Dead, - -	"	"	"	1	1	
Total, - -	2	3	3	26	34	

LAKE ERIE, July 15th 1813.

J Brooks
1 Mbr St

John Marshall Gamble

GAMBLE'S THREE SHIPS IN THE MARQUESAN ISLANDS

A choice between the harsh demands of duty and the melting appeals of Polynesian sweethearts — that was the dilemma faced by bluejackets and Marines of Captain David Porter's squadron in December, 1813, when commanded to leave their South Sea Islands paradise.

Tearful native girls, lining the beach, tried to swim out to the ships. "As a result of these demonstrations of love," an unromantic Marine historian has commented, "Porter's men behaved rather badly."

Porter managed to put down an incipient mutiny, however, and sail away with the *Essex* and three other ships. Lieutenant John Marshall Gamble was left behind with three small ships, manned by 21 sailors and Marines, to maintain an island base and fort.

In the spring of 1814, Gamble was overpowered and wounded by mutineers. Not knowing that Porter, meanwhile, had been defeated and compelled to surrender, by two British warships, the handsome Marine officer freed himself from the mutineers. After many adventures he sailed to Hawaii in one of the ships, with three sailors and three Marines, who had remained loyal. But he was captured by the British in Hawaii and taken to South America, where he gave his parole and saw no more action in the War of 1812. Broken in health, Gamble made his way back to the United States afterwards. Upon recuperating, he was promoted to the rank of major and then lieutenant colonel, remaining in the Marine Corps until he retired in 1834.

MANIFEST DESTINY

After the War of 1812, the United States burgeoned on land and sea with an explosion of energy. While traders and trappers led the way to the unknown West beyond the Mississippi, the merchant ships of the new nation sailed the seven seas. There were the usual cuts in military appropriations, which have followed every war, but the Navy and Marine Corps made the best of slim resources to protect seaborne commerce from piracy, which had grown to be a menace during the long era of the Napoleonic Wars.

The Barbary corsairs flagrantly violated the treaties of 1805, and Congress declared war on Algiers in 1815. Commodore Stephen Decatur was sent to the Mediterranean with a squadron of 12 warships. Marines in the fighting tops had a part in the capture of two Algerine ships and 500 prisoners, and the Bey needed no further persuasion to sign a new treaty.

From 1815 to 1825, expeditions against pirates in the West Indies took on the proportions of a naval war. No corner of the world was too remote for American punitive expeditions, and the frigate *Potomac* cruised in the Pacific for

The deck of the USS *Constellation* is shown in this photograph of 1903, when the old frigate was used as a Navy training ship. Marines had the duty of enforcing battle discipline over the bluejackets of gun crews. They were also expected to lead boarding parties and defend against those of the enemy.

several years, protecting American whalers from marauders.

The term "firemen" has been applied to Marines of today because they are so often employed as picked troops to put out a tactical conflagration. During the first half of the nineteenth century, however, the word might have been used literally. Marines helped to save Boston from a great fire in 1824 and put out a blaze in the Treasury Building in Washington in 1833.

During the period from the War of 1812 to the Civil War, the Marine Corps furnished contingents for navy yards and stations on the Atlantic coast and the Great Lakes. Recruiting was entirely on a volunteer basis. The pay of the enlisted men ranged from a private's $6 to $10 a month to the $17 of a sergeant major. The clothing allowance was $30 a year, and 15 to 20 cents a day was spent for rations.

A Marine lieutenant drew $25 a month, and he might look forward to three times as much if he aspired to the exalted rank of lieutenant colonel or commandant. But it was a long, slow climb, for promotion was by seniority in time of peace, and an officer often waited twenty years for advancement.

Educational requirements did not exist for Marine officers commissioned directly from civilian life. The intellectual side of the military profession had little appeal for leaders, who were seldom deficient in bravery or firmness. They enforced a harsh discipline over the men, who would not have respected any other kind, and both officers and men disapproved when Congress considered the abolition of flogging. An even more undesirable reform, from the Marine viewpoint, was the reduction of the daily grog ration on shipboard.

The fighting top of the Constellation, as shown in this photograph of 1903, was the station of picked Marines, who not only fired their muskets at opponents on the enemy's deck but also watched for an opportunity to toss hand grenades down an open hatch.

Various aspects of life on board a warship in the Age of Sail are illustrated below. A Marine to each gun was the customary rule of thumb, which meant that 40 to 55 would be the complement of a frigate. This was about one tenth of the crew.

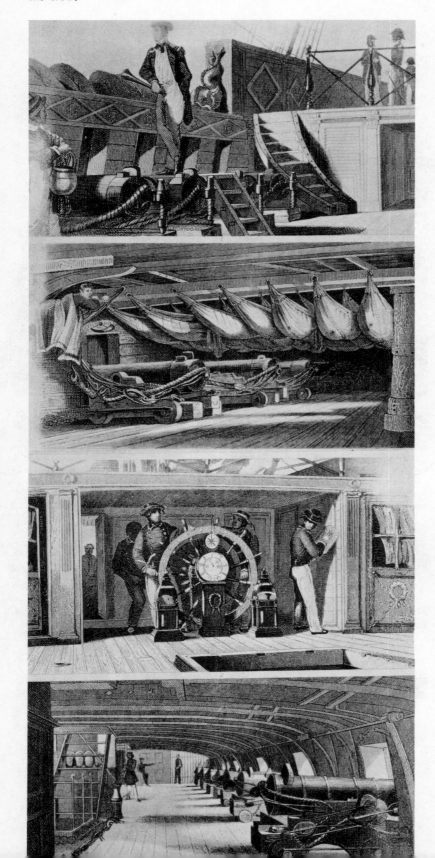

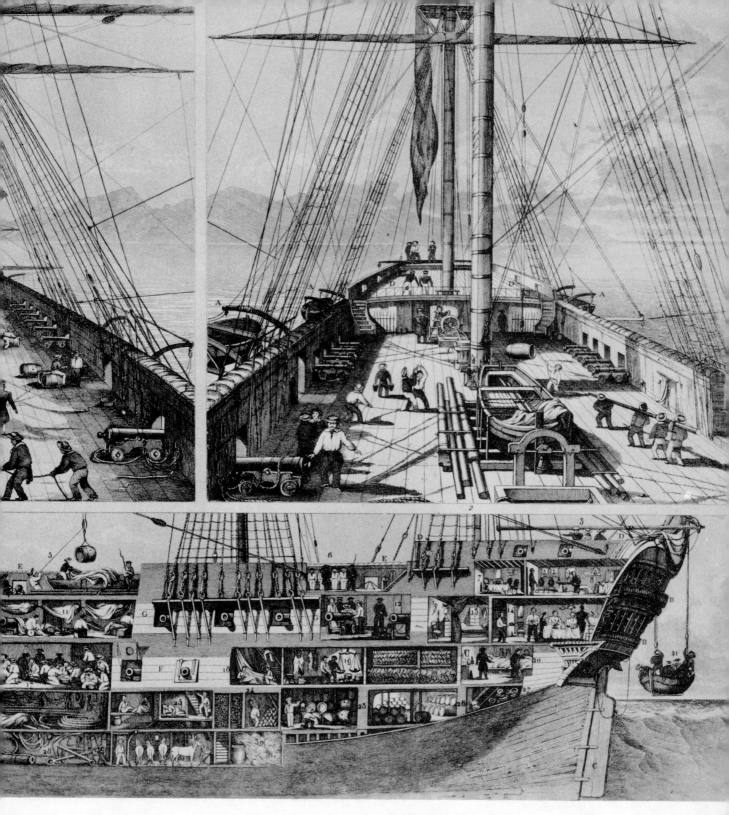

As these illustrations show, space was too precious to be wasted on board a frigate with a crew of 450 men. It took a tough breed to man the warships, and neither the sailors nor the Marines were gentle souls. Both esteemed their daily grog ration, and drunkenness was their besetting sin in port. Desertion was so common that part of a man's pay was withheld early in his enlistment as a preventive measure. As a cure, flogging was varied with such penalties as wearing an iron collar with ball and chain attached. But this may not have seemed a cruel and unusual punishment to Marines, who were accustomed to the high stocks which accounted for the ancient nickname of "Leathernecks." They took pride even in their hardships, and for diversion there were memorable fistic battles between Marines and sailors in waterfront bars. There was little love lost between them, though they fought shoulder to shoulder in amphibious landings.

55

Two fights of American ships with pirates off the coast of Cuba are depicted by contemporary artists. The upper picture shows brig *Enterprise,* capturing two pirate schooners in 1821. Below it is the brig *Alligator,* routing the pirate crews of three schooners with a hand-to-hand attack of Marine boarders.

No Peace for Marines

The United States remained at peace from 1815 to 1836, but there was no peace for the Marines of that energetic era. Expeditions against West Indian pirates were of almost annual occurrence, and one of the most lively fights of Marine annals took place on November 8, 1822. Lieutenant William Howard Allen led the Marines of the American brig *Alligator* in longboats to board pirates taking refuge in shoal waters.

On the other side of the world the American frigate *Potomac* chastised pirates of Sumatra, who had preyed upon crews of shipwrecked whalers. Landing at Quallah Battoo in 1831, 250 sailors and Marines stormed ashore, captured the pirate forts and burned the town.

An American squadron restored order at Canton, the only Chinese port then open to foreign trade, when Marines went ashore to protect American property from rioting Chinese. Not even the Fiji Islands were too remote; when a group of natives attacked the boat of Americans making scientific observations there, the Marines burned their principal village. Shortly afterwards two American naval officers were murdered on another island of the Fiji group, and this time a punitive landing force burned two towns.

The effectiveness of the little Marine Corps during this period was due in large measure to a commandant who has been a legend ever since. Archibald Henderson held the office from 1818 to 1859 — so long, according to legend, that he attempted to will the commandant's quarters in Washington to his heirs. At the outbreak of the Seminole War in 1836, Henderson promptly offered the services of a Marine regiment. President Andrew Jackson accepted and the Marine colonel led them in person. As progressive as he was vigorous, he made use of two forms of military transportation which may have established a "first." From Philadelphia to Charleston the Marines proceeded by steamship, and thence to Augusta by railway. A long march afoot took them to Florida for an Indian war ranking as a major American military effort.

The uniform worn by a Marine junior officer of 1819 is shown in this painting by a contemporary officer. The influence of the Napoleonic Wars on military apparel is evident, though it would not seem that this uniform was well adapted to duties on board a ship.

Notice on Door: "Gone to Florida"

One of the most delightful legends about Archibald Henderson has it that he simply locked the door of his Washington headquarters at the outbreak of the Seminole War in 1836 and put up a notice:

"Gone to Florida to fight the Indians. Will be back when the war is over."

At any rate the commandant led the Marines in a conflict which ranks as the major Indian war of U. S. history. Marine losses, from disease as well as enemy action, were severe.

Sea expeditions continued during and after the Seminole War. In 1843, Commodore Matthew C. Perry commanded an American squadron which landed Marines on the coast of Liberia to investigate the reported murders of American seamen. When the natives resisted, the landing force got the better of it, and Perry burned several villages as an object lesson.

During the age of Manifest Destiny, cannonball diplomacy was the accepted method of dealing with the "backward" peoples of the earth.

This portrait of Archibald Henderson was painted in his declining years, long after his Marines of the Mosquito Fleet pushed into the Everglades at the constant risk of being ambushed by the Seminoles. The commandant was 53 years old when he took part in campaigns which were a strain on younger men.

The landing of Marines and sailors of the USS *Potomac* at Quallah Battoo in Sumatra is shown above.

And below is an artist's conception of Commodore Matthew C. Perry interviewing natives in Liberia.

The Halls of Montezuma

Americans were more than willing to lend a hand to Manifest Destiny in 1846, when westward expansion led to a collision with Mexico. This war is commemorated in the Marines' Hymn by reference to "the Halls of Montezuma," though the storming of Chapultepec was only one of many fights in which the little Corps of 63 officers and 1,200 men figured.

Marines made amphibious landings in California and amphibious expeditions along the east coast of Mexico. They fought as infantry in General Winfield Scott's invading army, and garrisoned the California posts captured by Stockton and Frémont.

War hadn't yet been formally declared when Marines from the fleet landed at Point Isabel, at the mouth of the Rio Grande, to keep General Zachary Taylor's line of communications open while he fought the battles of Palo Alto and Resaca de la Palma on May 8 and 9, 1846. Ten days later a detachment of 200 Marines and sailors pushed up the river in boats and crossed with the first American troops to invade Mexico.

Commodore Matthew C. Perry commanded Marines who advanced up the Tabasco River in October, 1846, with the steamship *Mississippi* in the lead, followed by smaller steamers towing the landing craft. Three successful assault landings were made on fortified posts, but a second Tabasco expedition against new forts was necessary a year later.

In California, on July 9, 1846, Marines landed at Yerba Buena (present-day San Francisco) and raised the American flag. Both Yerba Buena and Monterey were held by Marines as the U. S. Pacific Squadron sailed southward. A Marine landing party took possession of Santa Barbara without a fight, and the occupation of Los Angeles and San Diego completed one of the most dramatic chapters in American history.

The climax of the war came with General Winfield Scott's advance to Mexico City in August, 1847, after securing Vera Cruz by an amphibious landing. On the outskirts of the city, Marines were in the forefront of the advance up the steep promontory of Chapultepec. Major Levi Twiggs fell at the head of his men, who continued to climb a height swept by a hurricane of fire. It took hand-to-hand fighting to prevail over a heroic defense, and the Marines paid with heavy casualties. Captain George Trevett led the pursuit, and his 46 Marines were the first to fight their way into the city, along with 20 soldiers commanded by young Lieutenant Ulysses S. Grant.

The frigates *John Adams* and *Cumberland*, the steamship *Mississippi* and the frigate *Potomac* are shown from left to right in the foreground of the American squadron that landed Marines at Point Isabel in May, 1846.

Contemporary artists have left pictures of two California landings. Above is a representation of the Santa Barbara of August 4, 1846, with the USS *Congress* in the foreground. Yerba Buena (San Francisco) appears below as Commander John B. Montgomery of the *Portsmouth* lands with 70 Marines and bluejackets.

The landing of Scott's army at Vera Cruz is pictured above, and below is an artist's representation of the fight at Chapultepec. Scaling ladders are being carried into action by the Americans making the assault.

On this page are two views of the amphibious expeditions up the Tabasco River. The Mexican War was the first conflict in which the new paddle-wheel steamships took part, along with the Navy's sailing craft.

MARINE ESPRIT DE CORPS

The Mexican War was a small affair when measured by the numerical standards of today's operations, yet it remains the principal military adventure of the nineteenth century for the Marine Corps. Brigadier General Henderson had imbued the Marines of 1846 with a splendid esprit de corps, and they made a noteworthy contribution to nearly every important operation of the two years, both in Mexico and in California.

Of all the Marine combats, the storming of Chapultepec was the most spectacular, although the amphibious expeditions up the Tabasco River called for more of their specialized skills. Paddlewheel, steam-propelled warships permitted more maneuver than had heretofore been possible, but even these vessels were rigged for sail. Not until the adoption of the screw propeller, in fact, did steam finally render sail obsolescent. Meanwhile, neither the Mexican nor the Californian operations would have been possible without American command of the sea and the ability to make amphibious assault landings.

先防戦士
常盤

Perry Opens Japan to Trade

Of all the Marine landings, none had such an impact on history as Commodore Matthew C. Perry's two missions to Japan. An artist's conception of the first visit, with U. S. Marines drawn up in two lines, is shown below. The Japanese prints on this page and the opposite page need no explanation, for the artist's perturbation is evident in every line. Even the American flag has a savage appearance, as seen over the shoulders of bloodthirsty Marines.

A hundred Marines, commanded by Major Jacob Zeilin, were first to go ashore in July, 1853, followed by a hundred sailors and two bands of music. Perry came last, with an impressive staff and bodyguard, and the Japanese drew up 5,000 troops to do the honors. It took a second visit the following year, however, to open up Japan to world trade.

It was a small world for the 1,400 officers and men who made up the Marine Corps of the 1850's, as trade followed the flag around the globe. Argentina, Uruguay, China and Portuguese East Africa were some of the foreign strands where the Marines landed. Their missions varied from friendly visits to stern visitations for the purpose of "enforcing respect for the flag," as it was phrased in that day of cannon-ball diplomacy.

The drawings on this page, originally published in *Frank Leslie's Illustrated Newspaper* of June 20, 1857, show Brigadier General Archibald Henderson and two companies of Marines quelling a riot. The occasion was an invasion of Washington, on an election day in June, 1857, by a Baltimore mob which had managed to seize a small brass cannon. But the 71-year-old Marine com-mandant was not intimidated. As frightened spectators scattered for cover, he strode up to the cannon with an umbrella for a weapon and pushed the muzzle aside. He had a narrow escape from bullets before the Marines dispersed the mob with a single volley. Several killed and wounded were left behind when the rioters broke and fled.

On the opposite page are artists' representations of two Marine actions of 1856. Protecting American interests in China required a fight worthy of being called a battle. Three U. S. ships, as shown in the upper picture, landed 287 Marines and bluejackets, who stormed the barrier forts of Canton. An estimated 5,000 Chinese were routed by the Americans, who captured 168 cannon. In the drawing of a landing in the Fiji Islands, Marines question natives accused of murdering shipwrecked American seamen. Several villages were burned.

John Brown Captured by Marine Detachment

When John Brown and his little band of followers established themselves at Harpers Ferry in an effort to incite a revolt of slaves, the Navy Department ordered Marines of the Washington area to the scene of the disturbance. Ninety were assembled on October 18, 1859, under the command of First Lieutenant Israel Green. They proceeded by rail to Harpers Ferry and reported to the senior officer of the Army, Colonel Robert E. Lee.

Some fighting had already taken place between Brown's men and a few volunteer troops, led by Lee's aide, Lieutenant J. E. B. Stuart of the U. S. Army, whose name would be better known a few years later. The result had been a stalemate: Brown had made a stronghold of the engine house, and Green was ordered to prepare for an attack the following morning.

Brown refused a last-minute appeal to surrender, and the Marine storming party attacked, using a ladder as a makeshift battering ram. After breaking down the door, Green had a personal encounter with the abolitionist, who fired a shot that killed one man of the storming party. The Marine lieutenant wounded Brown with his sword while overpowering him. Ten of his followers were killed in the "siege," four were taken prisoner and four escaped.

This ended the short-lived insurrection. After recovering from his injuries, Brown was taken to Charles Town, Va., (now W. Va.), to stand trial for his crimes. Only one verdict was possible, and after being found guilty of treason the fanatic was publicly hanged on December 2, 1859, maintaining his composure to the end.

Viewed from this historical distance, it hardly seems plausible that this grotesque escapade could have created such an emotional gulf between North and South. But men of good will appeared to have been infected with some of John Brown's madness. Such Northern intellectual leaders as Emerson and Thoreau paid tribute to the dead abolitionist as a martyr. He was even compared to Christ by extremists in the North, while being execrated as a cutthroat by Southerners, who viewed the Harpers Ferry fiasco as a widespread plot to free slaves and turn them against their masters in armed rebellion.

This photograph of John Brown (left) was taken a few months before he went to his death on the gallows in 1859. On the opposite page is a photograph of the engine house at Harpers Ferry, which the fanatical abolitionist and his little band turned into a fort. But the drawing depicting the storming of the engine house indicates that it was actually a trap.

Colonel Jacob Zeilin advanced to the rank of brigadier general when he became seventh commandant of the United States Marine Corps on June 10, 1864.

Marine Corps in Minor Role

Circumstances seemed to have conspired to reduce the Marine Corps to a minor role during the great historical drama of the Civil War. Brigadier General Henderson died in 1859, after half a century of forthright leadership, and was succeeded by Colonel John Harris. The new commandant, like most Marine officers of field grade at that time, was an old man. Not only did he lack resolution, but he was accused of wavering in his loyalties. It was the fourth year of the war, however, before he was replaced, after his death, by a more able officer, Colonel Jacob Zeilin.

Thirty-eight new officers, most of them inexperienced, were appointed to fill the gaps left by men who had resigned to offer their services to the Confederate cause. Congress authorized increases totaling 28 officers and 1,750 enlisted men in 1861, but at no time during the war did Marine strength exceed 3,900.

Rescue of Marines from foundering transport Governor.

NATION DIVIDED

The period from the election of Abraham Lincoln until he took the oath of office was a time of anxiety in the Marine Corps. Nearly half of the captains and two thirds of the first lieutenants resigned, most of them offering their services to the newly organized Confederate States Marine Corps. It was inevitable that the morale and effectiveness of the old Marine Corps should have suffered, so that the Civil War dates the lowest ebb of its esprit de corps.

A battalion of raw Marine recruits took part in the battle of Bull Run, suffering casualties of 44 killed and wounded. It was, according to Brigadier General Harris, "the first instance in [Marine Corps] history where any portion of its members turned their backs to the enemy."

No complaint could have been made of the 125 marines who destroyed arms, ships and buildings at the Norfolk Navy Yard after Virginia seceded. Another detachment of 110 Marines deprived the Confederates of the port of Pensacola by holding Fort Pickens until it could be reinforced, and the stronghold remained in Union hands throughout the war.

A battalion of Marines accompanied the expedition against Port Royal, S. C., in November, 1861. During the voyage the steamship *Governor* foundered, all but seven Marines being rescued by the *Sabine*. Reaching Port Royal after the fall of the Confederate forts, they served as garrison troops.

Marines were on board Farragut's ships at New Orleans and Mobile. They served on the *Cumberland* and *Congress* when those helpless ships were riddled by the Confederate ironclad *Merrimac*. And they took part in the attack on Fort Fisher, near Wilmington, N. C., in 1865.

For the most part, however, the Marines and U. S. Army regulars played second fiddle in a war fought by citizen-soldiers on both sides. Both the Federal and Confederate Marines were to recall the conflict as a period of tedious guard duty on ships and in navy yards; only at rare intervals was there an opportunity for action. After the war, of course, the Confederate Marines found their military careers ended. As for the Federal Marines, their numbers were reduced, as might have been expected, when the nation returned to a peacetime basis.

Young Second Lieutenant A. W. Ward, wearing the uniform of the Federal Marines, is shown here in the favorite attitude of youthful Civil War officers posing for a photograph.

The Marine Barracks, Eighth and I Streets, S. E., Washington, D. C., was headquarters for the small Corps of the Civil War. Marines marching outside the wall, as shown above in an illustration from *Harper's Weekly,* were a daily spectacle during the war years. Below and on the opposite page are dim photographs of Marines parading in front of the so-called "Old Center House," built in 1801 and torn down in 1906. Federal Marine casualties during the Civil War were reported as 77 killed, 40 missing and 131 wounded. The Marines had a high rate of desertion, as did all the other U. S. armed services.

CONFEDERATE MARINES

The Confederate States Marine Corps had some able young officers, one of whom, First Lieutenant F. H. Cameron, is shown in the portrait on the right.

Colonel Lloyd J. Beall was commandant of an organization with an authorized strength of 46 officers, 82 noncommissioned officers, 20 musicians and 840 privates. This quota seems never to have been filled, for a report of October 30, 1864, lists a total of 539 officers and men, in addition to three officers and 62 men who were prisoners of war.

The Confederate Marines gave a good account of themselves when one of their rare opportunities for action developed. They took pride in the fact that they helped to fire the guns of the *Merrimac*, though no Federal Marines were present at the famous five-hour duel of the ironclads, which ushered in a new age of naval warfare. For that matter, Federal and Confederate Marines did not meet in head-on collision at any time during the war. Both took part in the fight at Fort Fisher in 1865, but in widely separated parts of the combat area. It was one of the few actions for both in a war of dull routine duties.

Two noteworthy Marine operations of 1861 were the destruction of the Norfolk Navy Yard, as depicted above by a contemporary artist, and (below) the attack on Port Royal, S. C., ending in Federal victory. Although buildings were burned and ships scuttled at Norfolk after Virginia's secession, the Confederates arrived in time to save large stores. The Port Royal expedition is pictured here at the finish, with the Stars and Stripes being hoisted over Fort Walker, abandoned by the Confederates.

CONFUSION AND ERROR AT FORT FISHER

The principal U. S. Marine operation of the war was the attack on Fort Fisher. Admiral David D. Porter's fleet is shown above, and below is an illustration of the naval bombardment and troop landing. In December, 1864, the only important Confederate port open to blockade runners was Wilmington, N. C. On Christmas Day, 6,500 Federal troops landed while Marines manned many of the guns of the fleet. The attempt ended in failure, and on January 13, 1865, 8,000 soldiers attacked from the land side, while 1,600 sailors and 400 Marines created a diversion by attacking the sea face of the fort. The secondary assault bogged down in confusion as a result of mistakes, but the diversion enabled the Federal troops to gain the fort's surrender. Nine Marine officers were commended for their heroism, but most of the casualties of the Marines in the war were incurred in this fight. Recriminations were heard for years as efforts were made to fix the blame for errors.

Protecting Our Interests in Korea

After Appomattox the United States Marine Corps returned to its old routine as if there had been no four-year interruption. Expeditions to "restore order" or "protect American interests" in remote parts of the globe were of almost annual occurrence. Formosa in 1867, Japan in 1868, Mexico in 1870, Korea in 1871 — these were some of the Marine landings, with the Korean expedition attaining to the dignity of a naval campaign.

It is always hard to recapture the intellectual climate of a bygone age, and some of the chastisements meted out to natives in the name of "restoring order" seem harsh when viewed from this historical distance. But the Koreans did not stint on provocation when they burned a grounded American merchant ship and massacred the crew. And retaliation came as Rear Admiral John Rodger's five warships landed 546 sailors, spearheaded by 105 Marines, to storm the Korean forts on the Han River. The story of ensuing events is told by the photographs which are reproduced on these pages.

The Marines of this expedition were the first to be armed with the new breech-loading rifled muskets. Acting as skirmishers, they led the attack on the first fort, a semicircular redoubt. The Korean aim was incredibly bad as Marines and bluejackets swept on to take two more redoubts. This brought them to "the Citadel," crowning a height overlooking the river. The Koreans put up a desperate resistance as long as a man remained alive. Forty-seven standards and 182 cannon were captured at a cost of three Americans killed and ten wounded. Two Marines were awarded the Medal of Honor.

The Koreans had been taught "a severe lesson," as it might have been phrased in that day. But the results were not as satisfactory as had been hoped. Far from signing a treaty granting the United States trading privileges, the "hermit kingdom" held out for ten more years. Then a treaty was negotiated by means of deliberations carried on with the aid of a Chinese viceroy. But the Koreans still did not like foreigners.

This massive stone fort on a promontory overlooking the Han River was called "the Citadel" by the Marines, who stormed it on June 10, 1871, against a brave but not very skilful Korean resistance.

The photograph above shows the Marine officers who planned the attack on the Korean forts, and, below, some of the Korean dead are shown in "the Citadel," where they fell after resisting to the last gasp.

Mustaches and spiked helmets seemed to go together. At any rate, they were seldom separated in the 1880's, after the beards of the Civil War era had disappeared, and Marine uniforms generally showed Prussian rather than French influences. The Marines stationed at the U. S. Consulate in Apia, Samoa, appear in the photograph above, and below is the Marine contingent serving on the USS *Vandalia*.

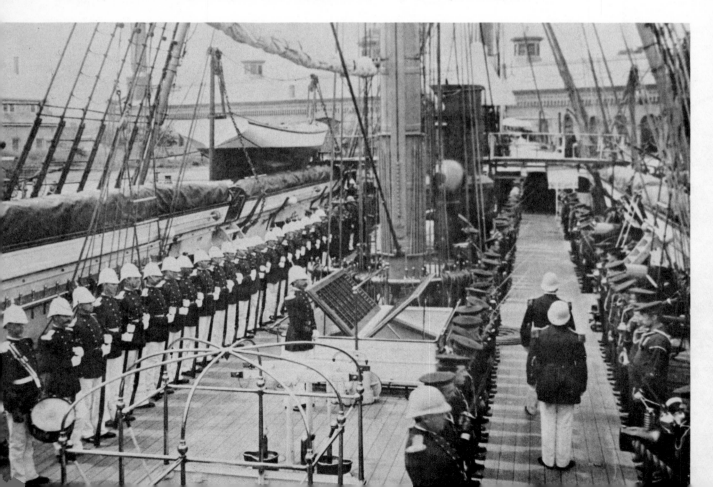

Spiked Helmets Worn in 1880's

Modes in military dress are set by victorious nations. After the Crimean War, French influences were apparent in the uniforms of Marines during the Civil War era and shortly afterwards. But after Prussia defeated the armies of Napoleon III in 1870, spiked helmets were worn by Marines.

The period from 1880 to the Spanish-American War of 1898 was one of the most uneventful in the history of the Marine Corps. There were the usual landings to protect American interests — Egypt in 1882, Panama in 1885, Haiti in 1888 and Nicaragua in 1895. There were other occasions when the Marines restored order in American cities during riots growing out of labor strikes. But a reaction against the military had taken place in an era of national expansion, and the Marine Corps was neglected, along with the Army and Navy.

Part of the Marine detail on the USS *Monongahela* is shown (above) while lining up for inspection.

In this photograph of June, 1889 (below), U. S. Marines on guard duty at the Universal Exposition in Paris, France, are posing in their dress uniforms.

SINKING OF *MAINE* DATES A NEW ERA

On the night of February 15, 1898, the battleship *Maine* was blown up in the harbor at Havana, Cuba. As events were to prove, the mysterious explosion did more than sink the *Maine;* it also put an end to a long era of Marine Corps history.

Ever since the Mexican War, the Corps had been jogging along, adequately carrying out a few repetitive missions with inadequate numbers. The officers were able men within narrow, practical limits, but it would not have occurred to them to study the theory of arms.

All this was changed as the nation clamored for war with Spain. A new age of naval strategy had dawned, and America's Alfred Thayer Mahan was its prophet. The United States was coming of age as a world power, and the mission of the Marine Corps was to be increasingly broadened. Officers of the future would have to devote themselves more and more to the theory of arms as all branches of the armed service founded schools for the study of military subjects.

The USS *Maine*, shown in a photograph taken shortly before the famous explosion, went down with a loss of 260 men, including 28 Marines. The ship's Marine detachment was photographed while embarking at Newport News, Va. Although a Spanish plot was suspected, no convincing evidence was found by investigators.

The officers who commanded the Marine battalion in Cuba are shown in the photograph above. Although officers still carried swords into the field, they were to prove more ornamental than useful in Cuba.

The photograph below shows the entire Marine battalion drawn up for inspection at Portsmouth, N. H., before departing by rail for Florida and embarking for Cuba with a mission of seizing a base for the fleet.

Marines Put into Effect
New U. S. Naval Strategy

During the 1890's, the United States suddenly awakened to the fact that a former preceptor at the Naval Academy was being acclaimed as the world's foremost theorist of naval strategy. His lectures at the Navy War College, published in book form as *The Influence of Sea Power Upon History,* were greeted with the deference usually paid to a classic.

These developments were embarrassing to Americans, who had been unaware of Captain Alfred Thayer Mahan's existence until he was lauded to the skies in England and France. But he was not to remain for long a prophet without honor in his own country. Theodore Roosevelt, Assistant Secretary of the Navy in 1896, was an aggressive champion of Mahan's doctrines and made many converts.

Where former writers had stressed battle maneuvers, the American theorist reiterated that the mobility of the steam warship was limited by its fuel. In short, the steamship required advance bases for coaling, and the acquisition of these bases was the ABC of naval strategy.

Simple as this doctrine may seem, it was charged with endless complexities in the transition from theory to practice. It was but a step, moreover, from the acquisition of advance bases to the building up of an overseas empire. Thus was the United States tempted by the possibilities of imperialism, on the eve of war with a nation whose colonial possessions were rebelling.

From a tactical viewpoint, advance bases had to be seized and defended in time of war, and the Marine Corps aspired to that mission. It meant that the old type of officer was outdated. Many of the junior Marine officers of 1898 were graduates of the Naval Academy. The intellectual side of war appealed to these young men, and the Marines were soon represented by officer-instructors as well as students at the Navy War College.

A month's field training at Key West pre-

At the right are the command and "staff" of the Marine battalion — from left to right, Lieutenant Herbert L. Draper, adjutant; Colonel Robert L. Huntington, commanding officer; and Captain Charles L. McCawley, assistant quartermaster.

Opposite is a photograph of one of the Marine gun crews which served on the warships. American marksmanship was vastly superior in the two naval battles and accounted for the defeat of the inferior Spanish squadrons.

ceded the embarkation of the battalion for Cuba. Marines were present with Dewey at Manila Bay and with Schley and Sampson at the battle of Santiago. But it is the seizure of an advance base at Guantanamo Bay that ranks as the outstanding Marine operation of the war.

After the battalion had finished its training at Key West, sixty Marines from the *Oregon* and *Marblehead* landed at Guantanamo Bay for a reconnaissance on June 10, 1898, and later that day the battalion went ashore with its own artillery. A Spanish attack in the darkness was repulsed, as was a second attempt made on June twelfth.

On the 14th, a vigorous Marine attack routed a Spanish force of 500 to 800 regulars. Sergeant John H. Quick was the Marine hero of the actions at Guantanamo Bay, which has been an important base of U. S. naval strategy ever since.

The Glory of War
As Seen in 1898

The Spanish-American War was an exuberant time which found photographs all too prosaic to convey the glory of war. Art came to the rescue of fact, as is shown above by a painting of the battle of Santiago on July 3, 1898. Below is an equally spirited illustration of the battle of Manila Bay, fought on May 1, 1898. On the opposite page is an artist's representation of the U. S. Marines advancing against Spanish regulars in the combat of June 14, 1898. But the triumph of popular art was undoubtedly the imaginative picture of the blowing up of the *Maine*, with the American victims plainly visible. It had a wide circulation at a time when "Remember the *Maine!*" was a national slogan.

ISLAND EMPIRE GAINED IN WAR

Small as the 114-day Spanish-American War was in the numerical scale, the results were far from insignificant. Almost literally overnight, the United States acquired an overseas empire in the Philippine Islands, Puerto Rico and Guam, not to mention an American military administration in Cuba. So well had the Navy learned the lesson of advanced bases that Hawaii was formally annexed during the war (July 7, 1898) and little Wake Island occupied that same week.

It meant that the Marines had their work cut out for them on the threshhold of the new century. For these new advanced bases in the Pacific and Caribbean had to be defended, and that was a job for the Leathernecks. It was a job that was eventually to lead to a new Marine mission.

Sergeant John H. Quick, shown in the upper photograph, is remembered as one of the legendary heroes of the Marine Corps for his bravery at Guantanamo Bay and later in the Philippine insurrection. The scene of the Guantanamo fight, as seen from the sea, is the high ground in the left center of the lower photograph. It was the first action of the war on Cuban soil, and after their defeat the Spanish forces in the Guantanamo area, estimated at several thousand men, gave no further trouble to the Marine battalion.

Shown in the photograph above are the graves of the three Marines killed in action during the combat in the Guantanamo Bay area. Total deaths from enemy action in the war were 18 for the Navy and Marine Corps, in addition to 439 for the Army.

Marines in shirt sleeves raised the American flag for the first time in Cuba on June 10, 1898, at Guantonamo Bay. Tropical heat and illness gave more trouble than the enemy, for American deaths from disease amounted to nearly 5,000 in the war.

PALM AND PINE

Until the novelty wore off, Americans took great pride in their new overseas empire. Everyone was quoting Kipling at the turn of the century, for dominion over palm and pine had become quite the thing in international circles. Nations such as Germany and Italy, having arrived belatedly, hastened to make colonies of such portions of the earth's surface as had not yet been claimed.

The United States had gone to war in 1898 to liberate colonies from Spanish oppression. Hence it was a bit disconcerting to be denounced in turn as an oppressor. There was unrest in Cuba, which made necessary an American "Army of Pacification." And there was downright rebellion in the Philippines, where the insurrection's leaders made it unflatteringly plain that they had absolutely no desire to be governed by the United States.

Meanwhile, there was the Boxer Rebellion of 1900 in China, and American troops had to be sent to Panama the following year to protect the canal, then under construction. This was only the beginning. As time went on, European nations threatened to use military force against Caribbean islands defaulting on debts. These islands were the strategic shield of the United States, and in 1904, President Theodore Roosevelt transformed the Monroe Doctrine from a policy of nonintervention by European powers to one of intervention by the United States. As a result of this "big stick" diplomacy, Santo Domingo was occupied from 1905 to 1907. It was the turn of Nicaragua in 1911, Mexico in 1914, Haiti in 1915, and Santo Domingo again in 1916. Most of these interventions took place during President Wilson's two terms.

A strength of 3,579 men had sufficed the Marine Corps during the Spanish-American War, but the demands of the next few years made necessary a force of 6,658 by 1903. During the two-year insurrection in the Philippines a brigade of 1,700 Marines was employed; it saw hard fighting and difficult marches through the jungle, such as the one shown above in a photograph of a column fording the Matian River.

Marines of the brigade in the Philippines are shown in these photographs. Among their adversaries were fanatical Moros, who fought to their last breath and made the Marines pay in casualties for any victory. It was a more serious war than the original conflict with Spain. More than 70,000 U. S. troops were used against larger Philippine forces, who took advantage of ideal defensive areas of mountain and jungle terrain.

Shown above is an international force, including U. S. Marines, forming a line of battle in Boxer Rebellion.

Below is a photograph of a Chinese mob looting and destroying Peking warehouses owned by hated foreigners.

Some of the Marines led by Major L. W. T. Waller to the relief of Tientsin are shown above, and below is a cannon captured from the Chinese. Waller reported that his men had "marched 97 miles in the five days, fighting all the way. They have lived on about one meal a day . . . and have earned my love and confidence. They are like Falstaff's army in appearance, but with brave hearts and bright weapons." U. S. and British Royal Marines fought side by side in the storming of Peking by an international force, and after the two-day battle, two companies of U. S. Marines remained on guard duty in the bombarded and looted city. This was the beginning of an era when every Marine veteran took pride in being known as "an old China hand."

WHITE MAN'S BURDEN CHAFES IN THE 1900's

Those responsibilities of empire which were referred to as "the white man's burden" in the 1900's began to chafe after a few years. It was necessary to keep large forces in the Philippines even after putting down the insurrection, and four battalions of Marines were sent to Panama in 1904 to restore order after a series of revolutions.

Marines sailed for duty on Wake and Guam who had never heard of those Pacific islands until they became American possessions.

Inevitably, the United States came in for unfavorable criticism in some quarters. The Marines, as the troops most frequently used for interventions, were accused of harshness. But, looking back from this historical distance, there seems little to censure and much to praise in the decent restraint which characterized their use of military force.

Even an ideal intervention, however, is hardly calculated to please the beneficiaries, and the best citizens of the occupied areas resented it as much as the politicians longing for a return to power and a chance to loot the state treasury. Both were likely to blame the U. S. Marines as the visible symbols of intervention.

Shown above is a 1909 photograph of President-elect William H. Taft being greeted in the Panama Canal Zone by Major Smedley D. Butler and his Marines. Below is a photograph of Marines on a troopship in the Canal.

First photograph of U. S. Marines on our new island possession, Wake, is shown above. It was taken by a "traveling artist," E. C. Rost, for *Leslie's Weekly* in October, 1899. Below is a photograph of a Marine battalion drawn up for inspection on a parade ground in the Philippines, circa 1901. The Moros proved to be fierce fighters, and jungle or mountain terrain added to the trials of campaigning "in the Islands." Early in 1902 an entire Marine battalion was lost in the jungle for several days. The rapidly vanishing food supply and exhaustion brought about a critical situation for Major L. W. T. Waller and his men. Ten of them died of exposure and malnutrition before the battalion was rescued by a relief expedition.

The Marine Brigade in Cuba

After coming into possession of Cuba in accordance with the terms which ended the war with Spain, the United States announced a plan to make the island free as soon as it was ready to form a government of its own.

Cuba was given three years for preparation. As a safeguard against failure, the island was reduced temporarily to an American dependency. For the Platt Amendment provided that ". . . the government of Cuba consents that the United States may exercise the right to intervene for the preservation of Cuban independence, the maintenance of a government adequate for the protection of life, property and individual liberty, and for discharging the obligations with respect to Cuba imposed by the Treaty of Paris on the United States. . . ."

This amendment was unwillingly adopted by the Cuban Constitutional Convention in response to American insistence. Four years of Cuban independence passed before the United States exercised its right by sending Marines to Havana in 1906, when bullets took the place of ballots in an election. They were the advance guard of the Army of Pacification, which served in Cuba. More Marines arrived until the brigade reached a maximum strength of 100 officers and 2,800 men in 1907.

The presence of American troops had a salutary effect and remarkably little fighting took place. But three years after the Army of Pacification withdrew in 1909, it again proved necessary to send Marines to Cuba. And by 1914 a Marine brigade occupied strategic points on the island.

This was the beginning of the so-called "Sugar Intervention," which lasted throughout World War I. It was 1922, in fact, before the last Marines returned to the United States.

On the opposite page is a photograph of some of the first Marines to reach Cuba in the Army of Pacification, 1906 — officers of the 2nd Marine Regiment, in camp at Marianao, Havana Province. It is noteworthy that they are wearing uniforms better suited to a warm climate than the blue flannel shirts issued to Marines serving in the Philippines. Above, on this page, are pictured Marines of the second intervention in 1914. Below is a photograph of men from this regiment on field maneuvers. There was little fighting during the Cuban interventions and Marines who took part in the campaigns regarded them as prolonged training exercises. Many of these same troops fought at Belleau Wood, Soissons and Blanc Mont in 1918. The practical field training they had received in the Caribbean islands was helpful to them in France.

Marines Land at Vera Cruz

Marines and bluejackets run up the Stars and Stripes over the customs house at Vera Cruz shortly after the landings of April 21, 1914. One of the American demands was that the Mexicans apologize for their conduct by saluting the flag, but they refused compliance to the end.

More Marine landings were carried out during President Woodrow Wilson's first term than in any other administration. The Vera Cruz occupation had its "incident" in the arrest of American sailors during the disorders of the Mexican Revolution. They were promptly released, but the American government demanded an apology. When is was not forthcoming, Wilson asked Congress for authority to use the armed forces.

The situation was aggravated by the report that a German vessel was bringing arms and ammunition to Vera Cruz. A Marine regiment landed on April 21, 1914, under the command of Lieutenant Colonel Wendell C. ("Whispering Buck") Neville, whose men bragged that his tremendous voice could carry as far as a field telephone. The Marines seized the customs house and advanced, supported by naval gunfire, into the city. Opposition took the form of sniping from windows and housetops.

Although the German ammunition ship did not materialize, the United States prepared for serious trouble in Mexico. A second Marine regiment landed on April 22, and Colonel John A. Lejeune took command of all Marines in the Vera Cruz area as they advanced methodically through the city, searching every building and confiscating firearms.

The hand-cranked Gatling gun and Krag-Jörgensen magazine rifle of the Philippine insurrection had been replaced in Marine units by the Springfield bolt-action rifle and Colt-Browning automatic machine gun. But riflemen still marched on their feet and Marine tactics had changed but little since the Spanish-American War.

Another Marine regiment was sent from San Diego to the west coast but never landed. U. S. Army troops to the number of 4,067 arrived at Vera Cruz on April 23, and the 3,141 Marines passed under the command of Brigadier General Frederick Funston of the Army. The resistance of the first few days having been stamped out, the occupation settled into an anticlimactic period of "watchful waiting," as President Wilson termed it, lasting until November, 1914.

Marine outposts, such as the one shown in the photograph above, formed a first line of defense in the sand hills west of Vera Cruz during the long occupation. The roundhouse, captured the first day, was occupied as a barracks by Marines that night. Later the two Marine regiments made camp in tents. War with Mexico seemed inevitable for a few days, but the situation soon took shape as just another intervention.

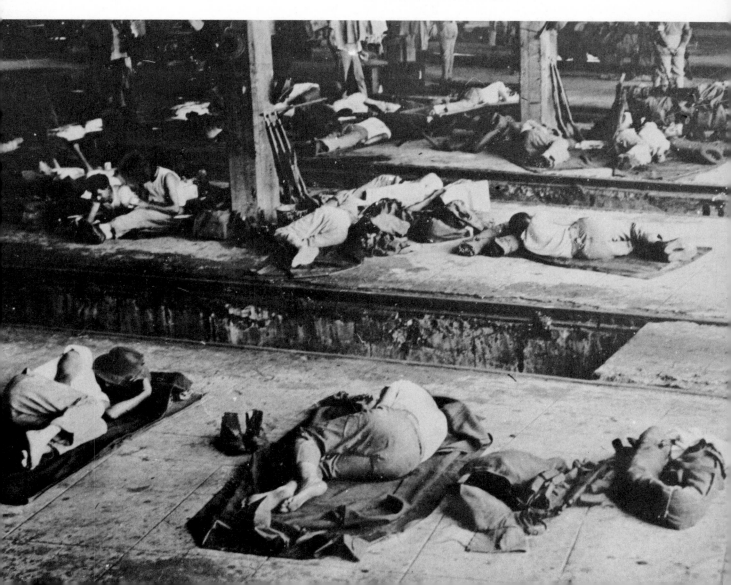

Marines of all periods have deplored a supposedly soft and degenerate present, as opposed to a vanished era of rough, tough Leathernecks. If there actually was such a golden age, the period from 1898 to 1917 deserves consideration. Then, if ever, rugged Marine officers such as "Hiking Hiram" Bearss had their heyday — officers who could march and fight with the best of their men in jungle campaigns. Above are pictured three Marine enlisted men manning the breastworks at Vera Cruz.

Marine officers had to make off-the-cuff decisions, diplomatic as well as military, which held serious consequences for their country. For instance, the occupation of the Vera Cruz area called for outpost and patrol duty, as shown in the photographs on this page, in a country aflame with revolution. Yet the Marines, led by two future commandants, displayed tact as well as firmness. And it was largely owing to Marine troop discipline that this "incident" did not involve the United States in an unwanted war.

When the crisis passed, the Marines set up camp at Vera Cruz and prepared for a long stay. The officers pictured in the photograph below are (left to right) Captain F. H. Delario, Sergeant Major John H. Quick, Lieutenant Colonel Wendell C. Neville, Colonel John A. Lejeune and Major Smedley D. Butler. All of these men were destined to make their mark in Marine Corps campaigns on Caribbean islands and in World War I.

Entire streets were pounded to rubble by rebel artillery in Chinandega, Nicaragua, during the summer of 1912. Some of the 600 victims of a massacre in León are shown in the photograph below. So bitter was the fighting that the rebels tried to stop a train on the way to León with Red Cross supplies.

Nicaragua in 1912

When Major Smedley D. Butler landed in Nicaragua with a battalion of Marines in the summer of 1912, he found a situation which bore more resemblance to war than the usual armed riots of Latin-American politics. The rebels had bombarded several towns with artillery and killed 600 people in León alone. So serious was the outlook that Colonel Joseph Pendleton was sent with a second Marine battalion.

Peace was not restored until Butler and his Marines stormed a hill held by an entrenched rebel army. Both sides opened the fight with artillery, and the Marines took the position in 38 minutes with losses of 4 killed and 14 wounded. The routed rebels left 60 dead behind. For the most part, however, the insurgents waged guerrilla warfare from jungle hiding places, where they could retire after their raids.

It was not safe for a Marine to wander far from his unit. Men who were captured by the guerrillas ran the risk of rough treatment and eventual death by hanging. The majority of the Nicaraguans welcomed the Marines as deliverers, but it was difficult for the American invaders to distinguish friend from foe.

A stone wall pitted by rebel shell fragments is the background for this photograph of a mounted Marine.

Major Roy S. Geiger, who was destined to head Marine aviation units as a lieutenant general in World War II, was the sixth Marine to be classed as an aviator. This photograph shows him at Pensacola, Florida, in 1916, when the total Marine aviation establishment consisted of six pilots and eighteen enlisted men. While other U. S. armed services were at peace, before and after World War I, the Marines had an opportunity to develop aviation techniques under combat conditions during interventions on Caribbean islands. Thus it was that dive bombing and air evacuation of casualties evolved, with tactical necessity as a parent. Air drops of rations, ammunition and medical supplies were made to Marines on jungle patrols, the aircraft being guided by a system of signaling which made use of colored cloth panels laid on the ground.

Noisy Nan, Circa 1911

First Lieutenant Alfred A. Cunningham, the pioneer Marine pilot, learned at the controls of "Noisy Nan" on the outskirts of Philadelphia in 1911 and 1912. Only "dry runs" were possible on this odd contraption, for Nan was merely a training machine. World War I gave military aviation its great period of development, and only a decade after the day of Noisy Nan came Marine DH-4's and DH-4B's, shown in the photograph below, lined up on a flying field at the Quantico base.

Twenty Years in Haiti, 1915-1934

Anarchy tempered by massacre had been the prevailing state of affairs in Haiti for a century when a brigade of 2,029 Marines, commanded by Colonel L. W. T. Waller, landed in August, 1915. The immediate cause of intervention was disturbances which had led to the landing of British, German and French forces the year before. And Haiti was important enough strategically to the United States for the Roosevelt interpretation of the Monroe Doctrine to be invoked.

The Marines had no difficulty in restoring order in the towns along the coast. The trouble came in disarming the descendants of escaped slaves, known as *cacos,* who had reverted to barbarism in the mountains. After re-establishing rail communications, the Marines found that only mounted patrols could seek out the *cacos* in the hills.

As a typical instance, Major Butler and 40 men made a six-day sweep of 120 miles through the rugged *caco* country.

Maintaining order in Haiti would have been an endless task for a brigade. But the Marines showed political as well as military acumen by organizing and training the native constabulary, known as the Gendarmerie d'Haiti. As a prerequisite, roads had to be built, economic standards raised and health conditions improved. Training Haitians to govern themselves was a task which took long years, but the result was stability and progress such as the Negro republic had never known before.

Rail transportation was the exception rather than the rule for Marines in Haiti, who depended on horses while patrolling the mountain fastnesses of the *cacos*. Medals of honor were awarded to two Marines, who penetrated into the hills and killed Charlemagne Peralte, a *caco* chieftain who led a small army of bandits.

This armored car was developed by the Marines for operations in Haiti. Anarchy and poverty were the real causes of the disorders, as the Marines were to discover.

Sure-footed little donkeys were found to be the best means of supplying rations and ammunition to Marine patrols in outlying regions during the occupation of Haiti.

A mounted patrol of Marines in a rural district of Santo Domingo is shown above. Searching the huts for hidden arms, as seen below, was a routine duty. There were no clashes which could be dignified by the name of battles, but ambush was a constant danger in terrain affording excellent hiding places.

Bringing Schools to Santo Domingo

Fighting was a last resort for Marines in Santo Domingo; they accomplished more by peaceful methods. From 1917 to 1920, Lieutenant Colonel Rufus H. Lane served as a member of the U. S. Naval Government in that troubled island. He held the imposing title of Chief of the Department of Foreign Relations, Justice and Public Instruction.

When he assumed office, there were schools for only 16,000 children, though 200,000 needed education. The money for new schools had been finding its way into the pockets of local politicians — the politicians who complained of Marine brutalities. During his three years Lane increased the number of pupils in public schools to 100,000 while cutting in half the cost of much-improved instruction. The Marine officer, a graduate of the U. S. Naval Academy, also did important work in revising Santo Domingo's antiquated code of laws. He died in 1948, aged 77, as a retired brigadier general.

This old stone fort, dating back to Spanish colonial days, was an attraction to Marines on the island. In some of the rural areas it was prudent for Marines to take their recreation in large groups.

Lieutenant Colonel Rufus H. Lane

"We Played It by Ear"

The Marines might have summed up their three decades of intervention in the Caribbean islands and Central America with one of their own expressions:

"We played it by ear."

This comment would have applied with peculiar force to Marine aviation, which came of age in the Caribbean island operations. Only a decade after Lieutenant Cunningham won his wings, Marine aviators had adopted necessity-born techniques of close air support for infantry, which reached maturity in World War II.

Improvisation was the spirit of the political as well as military decisions of this small body of fighting men, who had to create their own precedents in the absence of "school solutions." Before a native constabulary could be set up in Haiti, it was essential to grapple with the fact that 90 per cent of the young men tested had syphilis. Hookworm was so rife that a sentry could not be blamed for sleeping on post, and malaria had further debilitated prospective soldiers.

In order to wipe out disease, it was necessary to raise living standards, which in turn demanded better communications and economic conditions. The Marines were not social workers, but by the time they had made a military organization out of the Gendarmerie d'Haiti, the country as a whole had benefited.

It was inevitable that hostile critics of President Wilson's administration should have attacked the Marines, as did thwarted Latin-American politicians who were no longer in a position to loot the treasury. There were instances, of course, of officers exceeding their authority. A Marine captain in Santo Domingo committed suicide while awaiting a court-martial for brutality. But aside from such isolated instances, Marine interventions need only to be judged on a before-and-after basis. Where corruption and exploitation had been the rule, all of the occupied countries showed gains in governmental stability.

The Marines themselves profited from operations carried out during time of peace. Haiti and Santo Domingo were excellent training grounds for command, and the young company officers of the Caribbean islands became the field officers of the Marine Corps in World War II.

First Marine officer to be designated a naval aviator was First Lieutenant Alfred A. Cunningham, who won his wings at Pensacola in 1912 and flew in France during World War I.

Six Marine F4B4 planes, the aircraft of the second Nicaraguan intervention, are shown above while flying in echelon. Nothing seemed to be too difficult for Marine pilots to tackle in this jungle campaign.

OVER THERE

Americans flew to arms in April, 1917, with a fervor which derived in large measure from the fact that the nation had not known a large-scale war in two generations. The Marine Corps was swamped with volunteers. Before long the ranks were filled with educated young men, college and high school graduates, who would have been considered officer material only a few years before.

For the first time in American history, women served in uniform. As forerunners of the present-day Women Marines, 305 "Marinettes," as they were known in 1918, performed clerical duties.

It was a two-sided war for the Marine Corps. While the fighting was at its height in France, a larger number of Marines served on Caribbean or Pacific islands. Little or no recognition went to these men, for the words "over there," from George M. Cohan's famous song, were always understood to mean France.

The future Marines in the photograph below are not even "boots" as yet. They are merely recent civilians just arriving by ferry at the recruit depot, Parris Island, S. C. They have a long way to go before they can be classed with the Marine machine-gun crew (above) on maneuvers in France.

The tree-lined streets of the nation's capital were the background for this parade of Marinettes in 1918.

A familiar scene in 1917 — Marines of the 5th Regiment boarding a troop train for an embarkation port.

TELL THAT TO THE MARINES!

JAMES MONTGOMERY FLAGG

WANT ACTION?

JOIN U·S·Marine Corps!

JAMES MONTGOMERY FLAGG

Unprecedented heights were scaled by the lively art of the recruiting poster during World War I. This was especially true in the case of the Marine Corps, depending on volunteers long after conscription filled the ranks of the Army. Some of James Montgomery Flagg's posters became collectors' items a generation later. On these pages are shown two which doubtless inspired many a young man to enlist.

TOURISTS IN UNIFORM

Many of the Marines who embarked for France in the summer and autumn of 1917 had never seen the ocean until they reached boot camp at Parris Island. As for France, it had seemed as far away as the moon.

These men were tourists in uniform during their first few months in a foreign land. In their cheerful provincialism, they found the French "a peculiar race," but likable, despite their backwardness with respect to plumbing and gadgets.

Marines were reckless with their flimsy paper money, usually repaired with gummed patches. Shopkeepers of a thrifty nation did not fail to take notice of this weakness, and prices soared when a Marine entered the door. But turn about is fair play; the French soldiers who fought as our allies at Yorktown in 1781 had made the same complaint.

No peasant girl could complain of being lonely after the Marines arrived. And when they departed from training areas, there were tearful farewells.

The impact of the Marines on the French themselves could not be described in simple terms. They were amused by the insouciance of the newcomers and sometimes annoyed. And they were also saddened, remembering their own recruits marching off with flags waving and bands playing in 1914. So many, so terribly many, of those young men were dead or crippled in 1917, and still the war demanded more victims.

Training in France

When the United States declared war in 1917, tactics had not advanced much past the rough-and-ready procedures of the Spanish-American War. The French and British, as might be expected, became the preceptors of the Marines and other American forces when they first arrived in France. And since the Western Front had been immobile for three years, the Americans were trained in trench warfare, for a conflict that was to become mobile soon after they participated.

Sedentary generals of 1917 were fond of showing aggressiveness by praising the merits of "cold steel." Sergeants, performing as bayonet instructors, tried to inculcate the proper spirit by growling fiercely, "Suppose some dirty Hun was to rape your mother, sister or sweetheart, what'd you do?" But in spite of such incitations, few Americans ever saw friend or foe bayoneted on the Western Front.

Although the Marines placed a good deal of emphasis on well-aimed rifle fire, their European instructors regarded it as a business for specialists. Of more importance, from the viewpoint of trench warfare, were techniques of the machine gun, the mortar and the hand grenade.

Marine noncommissioned officers were taught at French or English schools for several weeks before returning to their respective outfits to become teachers in their turn. And in field maneuvers, French or British sergeants were often supervisors.

Marine training, varied with tours of duty in quiet sectors of the front, continued throughout the winter of 1917-1918. But when Ludendorff's last great offensive exploded in the spring of 1918, it was obvious to the Marines that the real thing had come at last. They were spoiling for a fight and they had not long to wait before they got all the action that even a Marine could desire.

Marine rifle fire astonished the French instructors with its accuracy at distances up to 500 yards or more. But the French regarded it as an academic accomplishment in view of realities of trench warfare.

Drill in putting on gas masks was held by Marines in old French dugouts behind the front, as shown above. Gas warfare may have seemed hideous to the people at home, but it was regarded chiefly as a nuisance by men at the front. Nevertheless, many "slightly gassed" victims died at an early age.

The war-wise old French sergeant in the photograph below is explaining the working parts of a grenade to Marines, whose campaign hats show that they are among the recent arrivals from the United States.

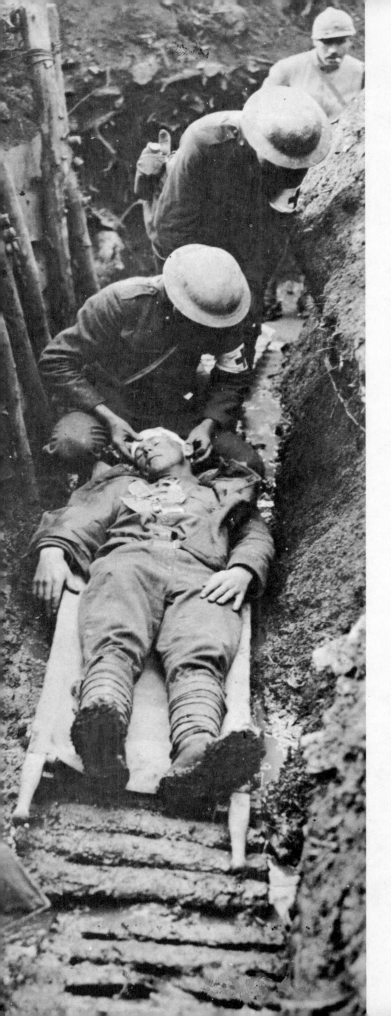

Moles and Hawks

Never in history had there been a war of such contrasts! There were the military moles — the footsloggers burrowing deep into the earth for protection against artillery fire. And there were the hawks — the pilots of the fighter planes in the sky above.

A common cause seemed the only link between them. Yet the men in the mud bragged endlessly of enemy planes shot down by aces of what has been called "the era of knight-errantry" in air warfare.

In reality, of course, the tactical relationship of ground forces to air was close. The planes were the eyes of the infantry, the artillery and the intelligence officers whose business it was to forecast enemy capabilities.

Up to the last few months of the war, the time, place and magnitude of practically every great offensive were revealed by air observation. The enormous supplies of ammunition for prolonged barrages had to be trucked from the railheads to huge dumps, which could seldom be concealed by the most clever camouflage. Aerial photographs of these dumps told the defenders everything about the forthcoming drive. That was one of the chief reasons for the deadlock prevailing until the summer of 1918.

A total of 232 officers and 2,180 enlisted men served in Marine aviation units, though only half of them reached France. The Marines, like all American fliers, were handicapped by the disgraceful failure of plane production at home. Despite boastful publicity releases from Washington, it was May, 1918 before the first American-built DH-4 — American counterpart of the British De Havilland — was received in France.

All of the early arrivals were defective. Warped spruce wings, short control wires, carelessly assembled Liberty engines — these were some of the lethal faults which caused the DH-4's to be called the "Flying Coffins." As a consequence, most of the Marine fliers had to serve with British units. Two won Medals of Honor and twelve were killed or wounded.

The military moles seemed the most earthbound when casualty evacuation was required. To the left is a photograph of a wounded Marine, with a French soldier looking on.

A Curtiss "Jenny," coming in for a landing on the Marine flying field at Miami, Florida, is shown in the photograph above. These were the standard training planes of all Marines, most of whom had a short course as compared to today's fliers.

The DH-4 of World War I, as shown below, was the standard combat plane for many years afterwards. With a ceiling of 19,000 feet and a speed of 124 miles an hour, it could climb to 10,000 feet in 14 minutes and could carry 1,200 pounds. One of the drawbacks of the "Flying Coffin" was the vulnerable gas tank between the pilot and observer.

The Marines had their baptism of fire on a June day in 1918. This is the wheat field that they crossed with heavy losses in killed and wounded while fighting their way toward Belleau Wood, in the background.

German barbed-wire entanglements at the edge of Belleau Wood were shattered by artillery fire when the attacking Marines began their fight to take possession of a rich Frenchman's prewar hunting preserve.

Hurricanes of shellfire reduced Belleau Wood to a man-made hell of tortured trees and ghastly stumps as the Marines of the 5th and 6th Regiments fought from thicket to thicket for every inch of ground.

"KEEP YOUR HEAD DOWN!" WAS CREED FOR SURVIVAL

Disillusionment was in store for Marines, whose adolescent ideas about war had been colored by descriptions of the Rough Riders on San Juan Hill or Pickett's charge at Gettysburg.

On the Western Front you attacked at a hunched, plodding pace under your load of grenades and extra bandoliers of ammunition. When pinned down by enemy fire, you hugged the earth as closely as you could. Even the gas mask over a man's chest, raising him a few inches, seemed to be hoisting him on top of a mountain peak ringed with fire.

The Germans had driven to the Marne, 35 miles from Paris, when the Marines were committed to the Château-Thierry front. Within sight of the Eiffel Tower, the fight for Belleau Wood lasted nearly a month before the last of the stubborn defenders were killed, captured or evicted.

Not many of the men in the Marine Brigade of the U. S. 2d Division were left alive and unwounded. For the two regiments had suffered casualties of more than 50 per cent.

Marine rifle fire proved itself in the fight for Belleau Wood.

The photograph below shows a German mortar crew hitting the dirt as an American shell explodes.

Marines pinned down by enemy fire in a wheat field are shown in the photograph above, and below are troops deploying for an attack. Veterans would say that they are dangerously "bunched up" at this stage.

BEHIND THE FRONT

Never did such creature comforts as a hot bath and change of underwear seem so desirable as when the men marched back from the front to a rear area. The horse had not yet been retired in World War I and the battalion officers who led the march were mounted.

As the mutter of artillery fire receded into the distance, the French countryside seemed sweet and fragrant — a land of flowers and birds and murmuring bees. Even the barns that were the billets of the men in peasant villages seemed cozy after cold nights spent in shell holes under enemy fire.

Marine veterans of the war will never forget the procedure known as "reading your shirt." Everyone became a host sooner or later to "cooties," as the lice of World War I were called. The best defense was a good offense, but they were persistent.

Fighting men bear no grudges, and the Marine sentry in the photograph at the right is looking on with interest at the card game played by German prisoners of war. But tours of duty behind the lines must end sooner or later, and the photograph below shows a Marine column halting for rest while marching back to the front.

Infantrymen still traveled on foot in those days, and ten minutes of each hour were allotted to rest periods. Marches of twenty to thirty miles a day with combat packs were not unknown in World War I.

As the tempo of the fighting speeded up, French camions, or trucks, took the troops up to the front in night runs. The Marines found that there was precious little to choose between marching and riding when it came to comfort.

But motor transportation made possible some decisive surprises by reducing troop concentrations.

Marines Take Part at Soissons in Cutting off German Salient

Men on the firing line cannot see beyond the horizon of their own platoon or company operations. Thus the Marines who attacked at Soissons on July 18, 1918, hadn't the slightest idea that they were participating in an operation which was to be the turning point of the war on the Western Front.

Ludendorff had shot his bolt with the abortive offensive of the 15th on the Champagne front. The French stopped him cold with the war's first extensive use of land mines, and the Germans were destined never to take another foot of ground in France.

Their successful drive of May, however, had left a salient driven as far south as the Marne. Its vulnerable flanks were Allied objectives, with the right flank, in the Soissons area, to be attacked first.

These tactical facts, of course, were not

The Marines depended on machine guns to repulse those hardhitting counterattacks the Germans were sure to launch in reply to the gains of an Allied offensive.

imparted to the Marines, who piled like sardines into the camions at dusk on July 17, for an all-night ride to the front. Their drivers were wooden-faced Indo-Chinese from France's colonial possessions. They had been trained to do one thing and do it well — to drive without headlights exactly twenty feet apart. The driver of the first camion was the only one who knew the route; the others merely followed. As for the Marines, they endured sleepless hours of bone-shaking misery, only to pile out with scarcely a pause and form up at dawn for the attack.

The best troops had been selected for this Franco-American operation. The Marines and the two Army infantry regiments of the 2d Division were in line with the U. S. 1st Division and 1st Moroccan Division of the French XX Corps.

Up to this time, machine guns had ruled the battlefield. But at Soissons, tanks proved to be the tactical antidote, as 356 of them overran enemy positions in support of the infantry. The Germans were taken by complete surprise and suffered a devastating defeat. And the Allies continued to hammer at the salient until it was wiped out, at a cost to the enemy of 100,000 casualties.

Camion travel was never famed for comfort. These Marines, however, are making a rear-area trip, as is indicated by their packs, holding all their belongings.

The second wave of attack at Soissons is shown in the photograph below, with the first wave dimly seen on the horizon. For most of the Marines, it was their first experience of attacking with the tanks, and armor proved itself in this operation.

General John J. Pershing, the "chief," as seen when visiting Major General John A. Lejeune (left) after the Marine officer took command of the 2d Division.

Clifton B. Cates, future Marine commandant, is shown in the photograph below as a second lieutenant, taking part with the 6th Marines in the Argonne fights.

Major Holland M. Smith, as seen above in France, was destined to win renown in 1944 as outspoken General "Howling Mad" Smith in Marine amphibious operations on islands of the Pacific theater.

This energetic figure, as drawn by Captain John W. Thomason, Jr., of the Marines in France, became almost an official emblem during the next few years. It was used on several recruiting posters, both during and after World War I. No other branch of the armed services in France was so fortunate as to have a fighting historian like Thomason. Taking part as an infantry company commander in the 1st Battalion, 5th Marines, he made notes for future books and their illustrations. Equally competent in both arts, he published *Fix Bayonets,* which became a best seller of the 1920's. In those pages the Marines of all the main battles are brought to life by both sketches and the printed word.

Thomason died in 1944 at the age of fifty-one, after seeing his beloved Marines win new glory in the Pacific.

Blanc Mont

Although Blanc Mont did not leave such a legend as Belleau Wood and the Argonne, it is recalled by a great many Marines as their hardest fight of the war. The Saint-Mihiel operation had been relatively easy for everyone concerned, but the high ground east of Rheims was vital to the Germans, who held it in strength and defended it to the last ditch.

Attacking from old German trenches on October 3, 1918, the Marines had Blanc Mont Ridge as their objective. Three days of savage fighting were necessary before the objective could be secured, and the Army regiments of the 2d Division had an equally hard struggle.

Two of the five Medals of Honor won by Marines during the war were awarded to men of the 78th Company for heroism in the Blanc Mont area. Private James J. Kelly dashed forward through the enemy artillery fire to kill a German machine-gun operator with a grenade, shoot another member of the crew and bring back the remaining eight men as prisoners. Corporal John H. Pruitt attacked two enemy machine guns and captured both with their crews after killing two adversaries. An hour later he was mortally wounded.

The Germans on Blanc Mont won the admiration of the Marines for their stout stand. Well supported by artillery, they held their ground to the death in many instances, refusing all opportunities to surrender. Their losses were estimated as high as 5,000 killed, wounded and captured in the immediate area of the Marine attack.

The operation was planned by a brilliant Marine officer, Major Earl H. Ellis, who served on the staff of the brigade. It was he who convinced the dubious French staff officers that the position could be taken by direct assault.

The loss of the high ground commanding the Champagne area meant that German preparations for a gradual withdrawal were thrown out of gear. Hasty retirements had to be made to avoid Allied flank attacks. But the week's fighting cost the Marines 494 men killed or died of wounds and 1,864 wounded, out of about 8,000 participating.

Enemy trenches in the Blanc Mont area are shown in the photograph to the left. On the opposite page is a view (upper) of the terrain as seen from the crest of Blanc Mont Ridge. Below are attacking Marine infantry under enemy fire.

The Nation's Greatest Battle

There had been nothing in all American history up to that time to compare in magnitude with the battle which opened on September 26, 1918, in the Meuse-Argonne area. Nine U. S. Army divisions, comprising more than a quarter of a million men, attacked at dawn behind an earth-shaking barrage by 2,700 guns.

The gigantic grapple was to last 47 days and involve practically every U. S. division in France. A total of 117,000 Americans would be killed or wounded before enemy resistance was broken.

Marshal Ferdinand Foch, generalissimo of the Allied forces, had been dubious when Pershing promised to wipe out the Saint-Mihiel salient on September 12 and be ready for the Meuse-Argonne offensive — more than a hundred kilometers distant in an area of poor roads — only fourteen days later. But Pershing's boundless faith in the American fighting man was justified when his nine divisions, six of them composed of green troops, broke through to an average depth of five miles.

This was only the first round. The enemy withdrew to a belt of defenses in depth, stretching back 14 miles, which included the "impregnable" Kriemhilde Line. Realizing that an American victory would mean defending the Rhine instead of the frontier, the Germans employed more than a fourth of their strength on this 20-mile front. Thus the Americans had to fight for every inch of terrain and pay dearly for victory.

MARINES AT FINISH OF MEUSE-ARGONNE

It was November 1, 1918, before the Marines got into the Meuse-Argonne fight, after being relieved in the Blanc Mont sector and filling their thinned ranks with replacements. But once committed, it fell to the lot of the Marines to make the main attack on the Kriemhilde Line.

As the photograph on the left shows, it was a matter of advancing through woods blasted by ceaseless artillery fire of both armies. Marines plodded forward in little combat groups, making the best of all cover.

By November 6 the Germans were in retreat to the northwest. But they were holding the line of the Meuse to protect the general withdrawal, and here the Marines had their last actions before the armistice went into effect.

Marine casualties for the Meuse-Argonne fights comprised 323 killed or died of wounds, 1,109 wounded and none missing.

The remarkable combat photographs on this page show two views of the same terrain. In the one above, Marines are preparing to jump off to the attack of a strong point in the belt of Kriemhilde Line defenses. A few of the assault troops can be seen as shells of the American barrage explode in the woods, which are the first objective. The photograph below shows the men scrambling up from their dug-in positions and advancing. Meanwhile the barrage has lifted to hit the enemy's rear areas.

The watch on the Rhine was kept after the war by men of the victorious U. S. forces, such as the Marine with a machine gun in the photograph above. The 5th and 6th Marines entered Germany on December 1, 1918, after a march through the Grand Duchy of Luxembourg. Occupying an important bridgehead of the Coblenz sector on the Rhine, the Marines remained on occupation duty in Germany until the summer of 1919.

MARINE ORDERLIES FOR THE PRESIDENT

President Woodrow Wilson was attended by Marine orderlies on the ship taking him to France for the peace conferences — a trip without precedent, since no other American President had ever crossed the Atlantic while in office.

The Marines assigned to him as orderlies were the envy of the Corps. It meant pleasant duty on shipboard, followed by an assignment in Paris, which the Marines in Germany regarded as the height of luxury.

As is always the case after American wars, homesickness was the rule soon after the armistice. Everyone wanted to start home as soon as possible, but any man would have been willing to put it off for months if he could have had Paris duty.

Not many of the fighting men ever got to see the enchanted city for more than a few days' leave after the armistice, although it swarmed all during the war with "rear-area personnel."

Marines and soldiers on a homecoming troopship could always "smile and look happy" for the photographers.

FLEET MARINE FORCE

With the great adventure in France at an end, the future of the Marine Corps in the 1920's was clouded with uncertainty. The occupation of Caribbean islands was not an all-absorbing mission. What, then, was to be the goal?

The 5th and 6th Marines had made such a good showing in France that one group of officers advocated the building up of an infantry *corps d'élite* as America's "Force in Readiness." Another faction insisted that the Marines were web-footed "soldiers of the sea" and that their proper employment lay in the development of advance-base missions — the training of Marines for the attack and for the defense of bases for the fleet.

Although some attention was paid to the seizure of bases, this was primarily a defensive doctrine. In 1910 a formal school for advance-base work was set up at New London, Conn. Exercises with the fleet were held before that date at Culebra, an island off Puerto Rico.

Upon this foundation was erected the mission which came to be known in the 1930's as Fleet Marine Force. For the advocates of ship-to-shore assault tactics prevailed in shaping the future of the Corps, and this was to have a decisive effect on the outcome of World War II.

AFTER THE WAR

The postwar reaction had set in, and the patriotism of 1918 was replaced in the 1920's by a spirit of unrealistic pacifism. Only a trickle of recruits responded to the posters, as compared to the flood of the war years. But since the shrunken Marine Corps was being starved for appropriations, the trickle was sufficient.

In the photograph to the left is shown a group of recent civilians arriving at Parris Island to be made into Marines by boot-camp training. And on the opposite page is reproduced a sketch used as one of the recruiting posters of the 1920's.

Now that the urgency of the war years had disappeared, the Marines had time to develop their famous and controversial system of "boot training."

No other American military organization has ever gone so far in heaping hard, exhausting drills and even humiliations of the spirit on recruits. The system is bound to make or break a man before long, yet even the most severe critics have found it hard to refute the Marine claim that a boot who makes good has a pride in himself and his outfit that is seldom found outside the Corps.

to Bill Matthews —
sometime 49ᵗʰ Co. I/5 Marines.
John Thomason —
1938

Advance-base exercises of the Fifth Marine Regiment on the island of Culebra, off Puerto Rico, in 1923.

Below is another view of the Marines hitting the surf and wading to shore in the Culebra maneuvers.

Ten Attempts to Kill USMC

In the 1920's, advocates of advance-base training argued that attempts to do away with the Marine Corps had taken place on an average of once every decade during the past century. The history of these attacks was summed up by a Marine officer, Lieutenant Colonel Robert D. Heinl, Jr., in a magazine article of 1954:

"If ever an organization has thrived on attempts to abolish it, it is this small Corps with one foot in the sea, one foot on land, and its head perpetually under the sword of Damocles. The battlefield and beachhead victories of the Marine Corps need no advertisement. Not so well known, on the other hand, is the Corps' durability in the face of ten successive attempts (all launched from within the U. S. Government) to legislate, administer, or remodel the U.S. Marine Corps out of existence."

Most of these efforts, the backers of advance-base training asserted, were based on the charge that the Marine Corps was duplicating functions of the Army or Navy. Hence it was taking a risk, they said, to stake the future of the organization on training as infantry — even as *corps d'élite* infantry.

Andrew Jackson set a precedent in 1829 when he recommended to Congress that the Marine Corps be merged in the infantry or artillery of the Army. The organization of 1,800 officers and men managed to weather this storm, but others were to follow, as in more modern times, when President Theodore Roosevelt fired a blast at the Marines:

"They have augmented to themselves such importance, and their influence has given them such an abnormal position for the size of their Corps, that they have invited their own destruction. . . . They cannot get along with the Navy."

In an executive order of 1908, Roosevelt took an ominous first step toward incorporating the Marines into the Army when he abolished some cherished missions of service at sea. During the next few months the Marine contingents were removed from thirteen major warships. But Congress came to the rescue, in the Naval Appropriations Bill of 1909, by restoring Marine service on naval vessels.

Altogether, nine out of the ten attempts to do away with the Marine Corps were blocked by Congress — in other words, as Colonel Heinl explains, by the will of the people. Nevertheless the advocates of advance-base training deemed it only prudent for Marines to keep one foot in the sea.

The Potomac River served for the simulated combat landings of the advance-base exercises held at Quantico, Va., in the 1920's, to put theory into practice.

New Training Methods in 1920's

Close-order drill became a relic of the past in the 1920's. Ever since 1660, when Inspector General Martinet of France made his name an odious byword, generations of hayfoots had been trained by methods which were retained at Parris Island in 1925 only for disciplinary and ceremonial purposes.

The lessons of World War I had taught the need for training adapted to modern warfare — body-hardening training, as shown in the photographs of the opposite page. Gas-mask exercises continued up to World War II, though they proved to be needless.

The Marines did not break with the past, however, when it came to emphasizing marksmanship with the Springfield and, later, the M-1 rifle. Long days were spent on the range, and Leathernecks took pride in their medals. Artillery officers attended the Army school at Fort Sill, Oklahoma.

REIGN OF THE D. I.

The drill instructor — or D. I., as he is known — has long been one of the proudest and most controversial Marine institutions.

He was not created. He has evolved, rather, from the drill sergeant of the days before World War I. But the D. I. is a more lordly figure; he is surrounded by an aura of divine right that the boot is not allowed to forget. It is his job to make a Marine out of a civilian in three months, and he is as dedicated as the chaplain.

Curiously, the noncommissioned officers who volunteer as D. I.'s do not receive added pay. Their laundry is free, however, and they are issued extra uniforms. This enables them to "look sharp" by changing several times a day in hot weather.

Histrionic ability is an asset to a D. I. He groans at the sight of each new batch of recruits with cropped heads. He swears that the bottom of the barrel has been scraped and he can do nothing with such dolts. Hence the boots strut the more when they are finally molded into Marines, as the D. I. has known they would be.

Re-enactment of Civil War battles was a feature of Marine training in the 1920's. These footsloggers are seen on the march to fight Antietam over again.

The Marines shown below were one of the teams of guards which formed an effective nationwide system of protecting the U. S. mails from armed robbery.

Wanted: A Mission

While the Marine Corps earnestly sought a mission, it undertook a wide variety of spectacular tasks. No other course could have been possible as long as Brigadier General Smedley D. ("Old Gimlet Eye") Butler presided. Never commandant, he exerted an influence on Marine activities out of all proportion to his rank.

The fiery Marine brigadier never lost sight of publicity values, and President Harding was induced to attend sham battles in which Marines re-enacted such Civil War classics as Antietam and Gettysburg. When the postwar crime wave resulted in robberies of the U. S. mails, the Marines landed on the front page again. They rendered a real service as 2,253 officers and men put a stop to the thefts.

Under Butler's dynamic leadership, Marine football teams played some of the leading universities. A climax was reached in November, 1923, when three trains filled with Marines made the trip from Quantico, Va., to see their team play the University of Michigan.

Marine embassy guard standing inspection at Rio de Janeiro, 1922.

Self-propelled machine gun, developed by the Marines in 1924.

Earl Hancock Ellis, seen in this photograph as a young captain, was one of the most dedicated officers of Marine history. As a lieutenant in the Philippines during the early 1900's, he learned to speak Japanese after concluding that the island empire would someday menace American security. Ellis returned from World War I duty in France to write a strategic plan for an island-hopping offensive in the event of war with Japan. A lieutenant colonel in 1922, he took a leave of absence and used his own funds to tour the Pacific as a supposed commercial traveler. Following visits to Japan and the Japanese-mandated islands, his sudden death from "illness" was reported by Japanese authorities in the Palaus.

Investigations were made, but the mystery of Ellis's death was never solved.

Colonel Littleton W. T. Waller, here shown in a photograph of 1915, was one of the rough-and-ready Marine officers of the early 1900's. Intolerance of all obstacles, human and inanimate, was one of the outstanding traits of this troop leader, who drove himself as hard as his men in campaigns which took him to China, the Philippines, Haiti and Nicaragua.

Brigadier General Smedley D. Butler, shown above with the mascot, "Sergeant Jiggs," did his best to mold the Marine Corps in his own image in the 1920's. Flamboyant and fearless, he was a good man to have on your side in combat. But discretion was not one of his virtues, and he sometimes embarrassed the Marine Corps with his controversial press statements.

Colonel Joseph H. Pendleton and Captain Charles H. Lyman, commanding officer and adjutant of the 4th Marine Regiment, were photographed at the San Diego Exposition in 1915. The principal Marine camp on the West Coast was named after Pendleton, who was beloved by officers and men for his ability to combine discipline with courtesy and good humor. Two more opposite types than "Uncle Joe" and hard-charging Littleton Waller would be hard to find in any organization.

145

Old China Hands

The creation of a generation of "old China hands" began on May 5, 1922, when the Marines of the Asiatic Fleet were formed into a battalion and arrived at Tientsin. They were given the duty of providing additional protection for the U. S. Legation while warlords fought for the control of northern China.

This was the beginning of "China duty," which lasted until the eve of World War II. Leathernecks who made themselves at home in Shanghai held the duty in high esteem. Never was there a time when an American dollar would go so far, or a place where an American enlisted man could live on such a lordly scale.

There were also taut and danger-ridden periods during the late 1920's and 1930's when the Marines in China might have been wiped out. That they survived was due to good training and discipline.

A mounted Marine legation guard is shown at the left, and below is a photograph of a Marine rifle emplacement in Shanghai, 1932.

Marine legation guards at Peking, as shown above, enjoyed a life providing such embellishments as White Russian sweethearts and Chinese servants. But there was another side to the picture, as is shown in the photograph (below) of a machine-gun emplacement in Shanghai, with its crew of Marines from the 4th Regiment. The situation became critical early in 1927, when American residents were endangered by the civil war. The 4th Marines arrived from San Diego in February and, before summer, reinforcements brought the Marine strength in China up to a brigade, commanded by General Butler. When danger from the civil war lessened in 1931, the Japanese invasion brought a much more serious threat. There were some tense moments for the 4th Marines on guard at Shanghai, but by one of history's little ironies, they survived, only to become the prisoners of the Japanese in 1942 at the fall of Corregidor.

Sandino's flag, shown above, was captured in his Ocotal repulse. Nicaraguan children, as seen at the left, favored the Marines.

Translating the "funnies."

NICARAGUA DUTY, 1927-1933

As compared to China duty, Nicaragua was dull for the Marine enlisted man — dull for everyone, in fact, except the dedicated officer or NCO. The seemingly endless routine of patrols in jungle heat was exhausting, and the danger of ambushes was constant.

One detachment of 150 Marines was surprised on a patrol in December, 1927, and lost five men killed and 23 wounded. The survivors cleared a crude landing field, and First Lieutenant Christian F. Schilt evacuated the wounded, making landings and take-offs in a cramped space. He was awarded the Medal of Honor for a feat that saved several lives. A quarter of a century later, Schilt was destined to be general in command of an aircraft wing.

Marines Learn Jungle Tactics

From a tactical viewpoint, the second Marine intervention in Nicaragua, from 1927 to 1933, was the most important venture of the Corps between the two World Wars. During these jungle campaigns some of the techniques of World War II were developed.

The trouble in Nicaragua began, as usual, with a revolt which quickly flared up into civil war. Leaders of the opposing factions agreed to a general disarmament and election, both to be supervised by Marines.

One of the rebel officers, refusing to disarm, found a refuge in the jungle with 150 followers. This was the beginning of the fantastic career of General Augusto Sandino, who made headlines in the United States by holding out during the entire intervention. A master of propaganda, he appealed to Latin America for funds and received large sums. He was even regarded as a worthy patriot by American liberals.

Although Sandino commanded as many as 4,000 well-armed men, he prudently confined himself to irregular warfare and ambushes. This was as effective a strategy as he could have employed, and it gave the Marines no end of trouble.

The Marines shown below repulsed an attack by Sandino on Ocotal. This defeat taught him to place his reliance on jungle ambushes.

No Latin-American insurgent, except perhaps Fidel Castro, has won as much renown as Augusto Sandino. Although he outlasted the American intervention in Nicaragua, his career came to a violent end by means of assassination.

Marine Lieutenant Christian F. Schilt (above) is seen with the Curtiss R3C which he flew at the speed of 231.4 miles an hour in 1926 — a feat so remarkable that it made headlines throughout the United States.

Rotary-wing Aircraft Tested in Nicaragua

The first rotary-wing aircraft to be tested under combat conditions was flown by the Marines in Nicaragua. Designated the OP-1, it was the Pitcairn autogiro, which could land and take off in much less space than was required by a fixed-wing plane.

The invention of a Spanish engineer, Juan de la Cierva, it appeared in 1923 as the world's first dependable rotary-wing aircraft, after the failure of many previous attempts by inventors. But the autogiro (originally a proprietary name, like "Kodak,") was not a helicopter. The engine of the OP-1 was used on the ground to start the rotor spinning, and for forward motion the pilot threw a clutch which transferred the power to the propeller. The engine of the true helicopter, on the other hand, is geared to the rotor at all times.

In flight the autogiro required the action of the air on the blades to keep the rotor spinning, so that forward motion was essential. But it could land "on a dime."

These tests were conducted throughout the summer of 1932 by a board of three Marine pilots. The OP-1 was put in competition with an 02U-1 Corsair biplane, which came off much the better. For the great defect of the autogiro, as the Marines saw it, was its limited payload. Fifty pounds appeared to be the maximum weight it could carry safely in addition to the pilot and co-pilot and 63 pounds of gear. This was far short of an acceptable minimum payload of 300 pounds for Nicaraguan operations.

Thus the first rotary-wing aircraft failed its tests, and it remained for the Marine Corps to take the lead in Korea, two decades later, in the development of helicopter combat techniques.

Although the autogiro flunked its tests, it never failed to delight the Nicaraguans, who gave it the affectionate nickname of "the turkey hen." Large crowds of curiosity seekers gathered to see it fly.

This Boeing F4B-3 fighter was assigned to the Marines in 1933. New aircraft were few and far between during those depression-ridden years of the 1930's.

New Amphibious Tactics Worked Out at Quantico

The reputation of the Marines for physical bravery has too often obscured the intellectual achievements of the Corps. For it was the Marine Corps Schools at Quantico, Va., which laid the foundation for American amphibious tactics of World War II. And these tactics opened up Africa, Europe and the islands of the Pacific to invasion without our suffering a major repulse.

As early as 1921 a brilliant Marine officer, Major Earl H. Ellis, foresaw that Japan would strike first and win initial successes in a war made inevitable by the island empire's ambitions. He envisioned a mission in amphibious assault landings for the Marine Corps.

Ellis wrote an operations plan based on an American invasion route from Hawaii to the Marshalls, the eastern Carolines and the Palau group as stepping stones of an advance on Japan by way of the Marianas and Bonins — essentially the route followed twenty years later. Some of his strategic ideas were incorporated into early ORANGE plans of the Joint Board of the Army and Navy (forerunner of the Joint Chiefs of Staff) for offensive operations in the Pacific.

In recognition of Marine advance-base work, the Joint Board, in 1927, gave the Marine Corps the mission of "special preparation in the conduct of landing operations." But operations in China and Nicaragua called for so many men that a start was not made until 1933.

On December 8, Navy Department General Order No. 241 gave official birth to a new organization, to be known as Fleet Marine Force. It was to have the responsibility for the seizure of naval bases, their occupation and defense. But the tactics had yet to be worked out, and that was the responsibility of the Marine Corps Schools.

Not much thought had been devoted to the subject up to this time. A Navy Manual of 760 pages, for instance, contained only five pages pertaining to landing operations. The Marine Corps Schools filled this gap by writing the first manual — a work later adopted to a large extent by both the Army and Navy.

Landing force exercises took place at Quantico to put into practice the Fleet Marine Force tactics being worked out in theory only a half mile away by zealous officers of the Marine Corps Schools.

It was a far cry from the first Fleet Marine Force landing exercises at Quantico to the training made possible by the amphibious base at New River, N. C. The photo above shows a simulated combat landing.

A 75mm pack howitzer is being wrestled from a landing craft to the beach as part of the training at the New River base. Here were practiced the techniques which led to victory on Pacific islands.

New landing craft had to be invented to meet the demands of amphibious techniques as outlined in the Marine manual. Above is shown an LCVP (Landing Craft, Vehicles and Personnel) in an exercise held at Camp Vieques, Puerto Rico. Below is a practice landing in heavy seas at Little Creek, Virginia.

With a Lantern and a Candle

Few people in this war-torn twentieth century are so simple as to believe that new tactical systems spring from some general's happy inspiration on the battlefield. They are the products of study and experiment, and eight years of preparation were devoted to Fleet Marine Force techniques before they met the test of combat.

The first step was writing a manual. Classes were discontinued at the Marine Corps Schools in Quantico on November 14, 1933 — a date which might be considered the birthday of Fleet Marine Force. The entire staff was given the task of committing principles to paper.

The head of one committee confessed that his group "approached its subject . . . about the same as every other committee, with a lantern in one hand and a candle in the other — but neither of these seemed to throw much light on the subject, so we wound up by hiding our lights under a bushel and using the imagination God gave us to use for this particular purpose. . . . We approached it with fear and trembling . . . fear for the aviators who put these operations into execution after we wrote them, and trembling for the troops. . . ."

An amphibious assault is neither a land nor a sea operation, but a combination of both. Thus it came within the province of an organization known as "soldiers of the sea."

Naval gunfire and strikes from carrier-based planes must take the place of artillery. The critical moment comes when the landing force is making the transition from one element to the other. As the men wade ashore from the landing craft, they are exposed to the enemy's fire when they have the least protection from their own naval guns and carrier planes.

Writing a manual for such an operation was pioneering of the first order. Yet the *Tentative Manual for Landing Operations,* published by the Marine Corps in 1934, was adopted with revisions by the Navy four years later as official doctrine. The Navy manual was incorporated in large part into the Army manual of 1941.

Landing light tanks along with amphibious troops was practiced in exercises held at New River, N. C. It took a good deal of doing even in a tranquil sea.

The United States was literally blasted into World War II by the bombs which made a shambles of Pearl Harbor. Never was the nation more united than on the Sunday when the stunning and incredible news reached the mainland. An appeal for volunteers by the armed services that day would probably have been answered by every able-bodied man in the country between the ages of 15 and 60. Nor was any sacrifice too great in coming months, although human nature asserted itself after the crisis passed. The patriotic reaction did not go unnoticed in other lands. Joseph Stalin, according to legend, counseled his generals before his death, "Never give the Americans another Pearl Harbor!"

In all history there has never been a naval disaster to compare with the losses inflicted by the Japanese aerial attack which shattered the Sunday-morning calm of the American naval base at Pearl Harbor on December 7, 1941. Above is shown the USS *California* burning while sailors and Marines make a futile effort to shoot down the invaders with rifle fire. It was remarkable how quickly groups of men from all three services recovered from the shock and did their best to fight back.

PEARL HARBOR

The destroyer *Shaw* is shown exploding in the upper photograph on the opposite page, and below is the battleship *West Virginia* burning while an attempt is made to rescue men of the crew. The statistics of the Day of Infamy are grim: Navy — 2,008 killed, 710 wounded; Army — 218 killed, 364 wounded; Marines — 109 killed, 69 wounded; civilians — 68 killed and 35 wounded. The Japanese losses were trifling in comparison: 55 airmen and 9 submarine crewmen dead or missing; 29 planes, one large submarine and 5 midget submarines lost. From a coldly tactical viewpoint it was a marvelously executed attack. The U. S. Pacific Fleet was knocked out in a few hours and left a mass of wreckage. But the Japanese were soon given cause to ask themselves whether they had won such an advantage, after all. For Pearl Harbor had aroused the American people as nothing else could.

Japanese propaganda photographs show Major Devereaux (above) being presented with a radio, and (below) the news of Singapore being read to unshaven prisoners.

THE EPIC OF WAKE

Some of the hurt and humiliation of Pearl Harbor were wiped out during the next few days by the fight put up by 449 Marines for two weeks on the tiny, mid-Pacific island of Wake.

From December 8 to 23 they beat off every attack. Bombed from the air, shelled from the sea, they repulsed landing attempts with losses to the enemy of two destroyers and a submarine sunk, three cruisers and three destroyers damaged. The 12 Marine planes shot down 27 enemy aircraft.

Elsewhere, there was nothing but bad news. Guam, the Philippines, Hong Kong — the Japanese were prevailing everywhere. Only on Wake did they meet with repulses, and the headlines on the opposite page give some idea of the prayerful response in the United States.

Of course, it couldn't last. The end was inevitable, yet Major James Devereaux surrendered only to save 900 American civilian laborers. The Japanese admitted to 5,700 dead and wounded, and their postwar writings reveal that the setback worried them.

There are few photographs of Wake, and the Japanese propaganda releases, as shown on this page, were intended to give the impression that American prisoners were well treated. It may be doubted, however, whether the announcement of the fall of Singapore was well meant.

Amphibian tractors taking troops ashore are shown above in the Marines' first large-scale amphibious landing. Below is pictured the landing of supplies which had to be manhandled inland from the beaches.

Guadalcanal

Many Americans had to consult an atlas when they learned that the Marines had landed on Guadalcanal. The time was August 7, 1942. And though U. S. naval and air forces had defeated the enemy in the decisive sea battle of Midway in June, it remained for American infantry to get the better of the Japanese in jungle fighting.

All that was changed by the Marines on Guadalcanal. The Japanese had not even the excuse of being outweighed materially, for the Marines were so poorly supplied at first that they had to subsist partly on captured enemy rations. The Japanese were beaten in down-to-earth fighting with the advantages on their side.

As an amphibious assault, Guadalcanal didn't amount to much. The Marines had a struggle after an easy landing on nearby Tulagi Island, but on Guadalcanal they were not opposed. The next day they occupied their objective — the Japanese airstrip renamed Henderson Field.

Two weeks passed in ominous quiet. Then the enemy landed troops and made a major effort to retake Guadalcanal. The Marines were targets for bombs and naval gunfire, yet they fought off the Japanese until reinforcements arrived to continue the hundred-day battle.

The Japanese corpses shown in the photograph below were half buried in the sands of the Tenaru River. They fell during a desperate enemy night attack which failed to shake the Marine hold on Guadalcanal.

A Marine patrol up the shallow Tenaru River, as shown in the photograph to the left, accomplished its mission of destroying two Japanese 75mm fieldpieces. In the photograph below, Marines are carrying a wounded comrade to safety in a forest area exposed to the fire of concealed Japanese snipers. There were no encounters on the heroic scale of a battle in the Guadalcanal campaign. It was simply a warfare of deadly attrition, with the enemy specializing in night attacks and the Marines in daytime patrols. Malaria fought against both forces.

The Shadow Before

The significance of Guadalcanal could not have been recognized by outweighed Marines, such as those pictured below, battling to keep from being overwhelmed. Not until months later would it be apparent that this island of the Solomon group was the farthest point of advance for the enemy drive southward, which had begun in December, 1941. At Guadalcanal, for the first time, the Japanese were stopped on land. They were stopped by Americans who had been civilians for the most part on the day of Pearl Harbor, never dreaming that they would soon be volunteers in a Marine uniform. Thus the Japanese lost more than an island with a half-finished airfield. They lost a legend of invincibility they had believed in fanatically up to that time.

THE TURNING POINT

The first twenty days of November, 1942, were the turning point not only on Guadalcanal but also in the world-wide struggle against the Axis powers. The Germans were stopped at Stalingrad; they and their Italian allies were beaten at El Alamein in the Libyan desert; and American forces staged history's greatest amphibious assault landing in northwest Africa.

Guadalcanal seems insignificant in comparison to these earth-shaking events. Yet the long struggle on this island ended with the Japanese on the strategic offensive, even as Germany and Italy in their theaters of operation.

Returning to the tactical level, the photograph at the left shows a Marine loading ammunition into machine-gun belts in preparation for the next encounter on Guadalcanal. The terrain consists of tall grass as well as jungle, and the photograph below gives a view of a single-file Marine column advancing.

Henderson Field demonstrated that it was worth a hard fight when Marine and Navy planes had a decisive part in the terrific sea battles fought in nearby waters. While Major General Alexander A. Vandegrift's footsloggers inched their way forward in the jungle, Marine bombing planes were droning overhead on their way to sink transports bringing Japanese reinforcements. The photograph above shows a former enemy building which Marine and Navy airmen made a headquarters. On the right is a view of a bridge thrown across the Matanikau River by U. S. Seabees, who had forgotten the word "impossible." And below is a Marine TBF and its load of 500-pound bombs.

This Was Tarawa

Marine amphibious tactics had been given their greatest test, up to the fall of 1943, by U. S. Army assault landings in northwest Africa and Sicily. Three of the participating Army divisions had received training from the Marines in ship-to-shore assault landing techniques before leaving this country.

The Army in its turn had made a special study of shore-to-shore amphibious landings which paid off in the coin of victory as General Douglas MacArthur's forces worked their way up the shore line of New Guinea, sealing off Japanese troops to "wither on the vine." It was an economical way of making war, and the Army had developed an amphibious vehicle in the "duck" (from DukW, a designation meaning precisely nothing), which the Marines promptly adopted.

Amphibious tactics had prevailed everywhere up to November, 1943, when the Marines landed on Bougainville and in the Gilberts. Then a landing came perilously near to defeat, and the name of that disaster was Tarawa. It made no

difference that the actual point of attack was Betio Island; the word "Tarawa" (the name of the atoll) became the symbol of a slaughter calling for a re-evaluation of Marine techniques.

The final figures of 984 killed and 2,072 wounded were small in comparison to casualties on the Russian front. But a man is a man in the Marines, not a unit of a mass of cannon fodder. Hundreds of Marines were cut down in the surf before the survivors won a foothold. But within a week they were in control of the Gilberts, after killing the entire garrison of 4,000 Japanese, with the exception of 146 who surrendered.

Exhaustive studies made it clear that previous estimates of the air strikes and naval gunfire required to "soften up" an objective would have to be revised upward. The Japanese had proved that concrete emplacements could withstand an unbelievable amount of pounding.

The tactical antidote, as the Marines saw it, was better reconnaissance and planning, followed by more intensive preliminary fire.

On these two pages are combat photographs of the Marines who fought for life on Tarawa Atoll after surviving the slaughter in the surf. Men lived only by taking advantage of every scrap of cover. And in the end the dogged courage of recent American civilians prevailed over Japanese fanaticism.

THE MARSHALLS

The harsh lessons of Tarawa were applied so intelligently in the Marshalls that those islands were overrun in a thrifty Marine and Army operation.

Major General Holland M. ("Howling Mad") Smith and Major General Julian C. Smith, the Marine commanders at Tarawa, had concluded that there was no such thing as too much "preparation." Every enemy installation above ground must be pounded into rubble, and that is what happened to the two main' objectives in the Marshalls after two days of naval gunfire and strikes by land-based planes.

More amphibian tractors were provided to avoid losses such as those in the surf at Tarawa. As a result, Roi, Namur and Eniwetok, in Kwajalein Atoll of the Marshalls, were taken in February, 1944, at half the cost of Tarawa. Thus the outer barrier of Japan's island defenses was breached.

Preliminary strikes by Marine land-based TBM aircraft (opposite page) left a trail of 1,000-pound bombs drifting earthward through cloud castles in the sky to explode on islands of Kwajalein Atoll in the Marshalls.

Naval gunfire, as show in the photograph of the battleship *Idaho* pouring it in at point-blank range with her 14-inch rifles, left a scene of savage desolation on the main objectives of Marine attack.

Even so, there was plenty of work left for the infantry of the landing forces, as the photographs on these pages will testify. For the Japanese resisted in their underground installations until the last man was killed.

The Seizure of Saipan Opens Japan to Bombing

War, said Clausewitz, is a trinity of violence, chance and reason. In other words, nothing is ever certain in war as long as the human element is present, not to mention such imponderables as weather and terrain. But in the spring of 1944, with Saipan looming as the next objective, Marine amphibious tactics had been reduced as nearly as possible to a science.

Even so, there were always such unpredictables as the disaster at Pearl Harbor in which an LST blew up while loading ammunition for the Saipan operation. The explosion set fire to five other LSTs, with a loss of 200 sailors and Marines.

Rehearsals were held on the island of Maui in the Hawaiian group. On June 8 the armada of 775 warships and transports rendezvoused at Eniwetok in the Marshalls. There the 100,000 Army and Marine troops and 250,000 sailors heard the news that a tremendous Anglo-American amphibious landing had succeeded in Normandy.

Marine generals knew that the price of victory on Saipan would not be cheap. Too large to be taken at a tactical gulp and too small for maneuver, the island is twelve miles long by five and a half wide. It abounds in ridges, valleys and caves. The Japanese would be sure to defend these to the death.

But if ever an objective was worth a calculated risk, it was Saipan. For its seizure would put land-based U. S. bombers within range of Japan for the first time in the war.

The enemy had not overlooked this possibility and 29,662 dug-in Japanese gave 77,143 attackers (one Army and two Marine divisions) a terrific fight. Both sides were supported by artillery, armor and air strikes. It took 24 days for Saipan to be secured, and the victors suffered 3,143 killed, 335 missing and 13,208 wounded, most of them Marines. Japanese losses were 23,143 dead and 1,810 prisoners. At the finish, hundreds of Japanese civilians leaped from a cliff in a mass suicide.

MARINES WHO PAID WITH THEIR LIVES

On these pages are photographs showing the reverse side of the victory medal — the Marines who paid with their lives, or suffered maiming wounds.

Nothing had been stinted to give these men the best support possible. The Marine fighter-bomber Corsair, as shown on Page 168, pursued the Japanese into the hills on Saipan and scorched them out of their caves with rockets. Marine tanks and artillery backed the assault troops to the limit. But someone has to pay when the going is rough, and the wooden memorial to an unknown Marine on Saipan attests to the inevitable.

Sometimes a Marine got no farther than the landing beach, itself, and a rifle stuck in the sand was his memorial for the time being. But the Marines pride themselves on taking care of their wounded at any risk, and below is shown a casualty being evacuated for a long flight to a base hospital.

Marine tanks and infantry gave each other needed support on Saipan, as shown in the photograph above. The assault troops were driving inland from the beach, where they were hit hard by enemy fire.

Every square yard of terrain had to be searched for hidden Japanese foemen as the Marines fought their way slowly to the interior of the island. And it was seldom indeed that an enemy ever surrendered.

The tense face of combat is seen in the photograph above, and on the right is a picture of a Marine at the instant he was hit by fragments from the enemy mortar shell exploding in the background. Below is an action shot of a Marine bazooka team attempting to knock out a Japanese roadblock. Only by this kind of toe-to-toe slugging could the assault troops win in a campaign of sheer attrition.

Guam and Tinian, the remaining large islands of the Marianas group, were next after the securing of Saipan. Guam, having been taken from us during the first week of the war in the Pacific, was our first reconquest. Shown above is the scene of seeming bedlam on the beach, and below is a view of the jungle fighting as the troops drove inland. It took a campaign of twenty days in July and August, 1944, to put down all resistance. The cost to Marine and Army troops was 1,919 killed and 7,122 wounded.

GUAM AND TINIAN, TWIN OPERATIONS

The lessons of Saipan were put into effect on Guam and Tinian, attacked on July 21 and 24 respectively. But it took until August 10 to secure Guam, while all serious resistance on Tinian ended in a week.

Tinian was the first Marine shore-to-shore operation. The assault troops crossed the narrow strait separating the island from Saipan and took the defenders by surprise, landing on a beach the Japanese considered too cramped to be taken seriously in their plans.

Above on this page is a view of Marines advancing under an angry sky, and below is a mopping-up group at the finish. On Tinian the new napalm bombs, made of jellied gasoline, were used for the first time with terrible effect on enemy positions.

Hell on Peleliu for the Marines

Peleliu, about six miles long and two wide, was just large enough to provide the Japanese with a maze of underground hiding places, and small enough to afford the Marines very little cover. It was hell for 27 days before they finally secured one of the most repellent pieces of real estate on earth.

The Palaus, of which Peleliu is one of the smaller islands, lie 530 miles south of the southern Philippines. The purpose of the American attack was to seize an air base for the advance to the Philippines. As it happened, MacArthur landed on Leyte just a week after the securing of Peleliu, bringing up the question of whether the island was worth the 1,241 Marine dead it cost.

Never had the Marines gone up against such a defensive system as the limestone caves in the ridges of Peleliu. Some of them were six

The heat on Peleliu was terrific. Above is shown a Marine giving a wounded comrade a drink of water, and below are the landing craft on D day — September 15, 1944.

174

"stories" deep, with several entrances, connected by tunnels. Armored doors opened long enough for a fieldpiece to fire, then closed automatically. There were slits for machine-gun fire.

Thus the Marines faced the tactical problem of exterminating 11,000 foemen determined to resist to the death. Naval guns pounded the ridges and Marine Corsairs blasted the caves with 1,000-pound bombs and napalm, hoping to seal them off or burn up the oxygen.

Day after day the struggle went on in heat over a hundred degrees. There was no easy way to victory on Peleliu, and the fight for Bloody Nose Ridge was worst of all.

The beaches on Peleliu were mined and the Marines had heavy losses on D day. Shells from Japanese caves hit men unloading supplies.

This is Peleliu as it appeared to the Marines going in on landing craft — a man-made hell of smoke and flame. When the island could be seen, it combined a mangrove swamp and second-rate airstrip with tortured ridges covered by thorny bushes and stunted trees.

The inevitable island — that name was aptly applied to Iwo Jima. For it was midway between Japan and the bases of the American B-29s on Saipan and Tinian. And its seizure would provide the large bombers with a way station if they limped home damaged from Japanese anti-aircraft guns. Unfortunately for the attackers, the enemy was aware of the potential importance of this tiny outpost, five miles long by two and a half wide, with a dead volcano named Mount Suribachi at its southern tip. By August, 1944, the entire island had been made into a fort, with concrete emplacements and underground installations for 22,000 Japanese, and arms ranging from machine guns to mortars and 155mm howitzers.

Iwo Jima

This was the big one — this was Iwo! When you had been through Iwo, you had seen men taking all a human being could stand. The landing craft going in, with Suribachi in the distance, are shown in the upper photograph. Below are two views of the men hitting the beaches. The coarse-grained black volcanic sand was an impediment to walking, but the enemy did not defend the beaches. His plan called for luring the Marines into fields of fire so cunningly contrived that it seemed nothing could live. D-day was February 19, 1945 and Iwo Jima was not secured until March 26. The Marines lost a total of 4,644 dead and 17,328 wounded in 35 days of unrelenting combat.

Another view of Marines on the beach is shown in the photograph above, and below are pictured men advancing against unseen opponents, with Mount Suribachi an objective at the island's southern tip.

Man Trap

The quick and the dead on Iwo were separated only by an inch of space and a second of time. For the bullet that missed you may have killed the man behind you. The photographs on this page show the advance to the interior of the island, where enemy resistance seemed to grow stiffer with every yard. The Japanese on Iwo intended to sell their lives dearly, and there were no "banzai charges." The enemy meant business on Iwo and he made the Marines pay for every inch of coarse black sand.

The northern end of Iwo, where
the enemy made his last stand,
consists of rugged terrain with rocky
ridges as well as hills of sand.
Here the Japanese were protected
by caves and emplacements of concrete thirty inches thick. The attackers had to go up against these
positions, supported by tanks and
flame-throwers. Often enough, however, it was a footslogger's grenade
that killed the last defender. Years
later some of the sealed-off Japanese caves were found, the bodies in
them preserved by the sulphur which
was Iwo's only product.

Okinawa

On Easter Sunday, 1945, the first Marine and Army amphibian tractors hit the beaches of Okinawa without a shot being fired at them. The calm was ominous, for everyone knew that the enemy would put up a fight for this large island. Okinawa was obviously the springboard for an American advance on Japan and it was not secured until June 22, with American casualties of 48,025 killed and wounded. Most of the losses were suffered by the Navy as a result of Japanese kamikaze attacks. The Marines reported 2,834 killed and 13,523 wounded. It was their last large-scale action of the war.

Sixty-seven miles long, with 450,000 inhabitants, Okinawa was large enough to afford elbow room for the American forces to maneuver. On this page are shown Marines in two typical infantry combat scenes.

A Marine Corsair, tailed by a P-38 photo plane, drops a fire bomb on an enemy position in the Okinawa mountains. The infantry had excellent close air support from Marine aircraft throughout the Okinawa fights.

Marine wounded, as seen in the photograph below, are being placed in an amphibian tractor for evacuation while the infantry advances along the sea wall. The Japanese defenses were well organized everywhere.

Wana Ridge, covering the key enemy position at Shuri, was the objective of the Marines in the photographs shown on this page. The enemy counterattacked at every opportunity, sometimes regaining lost ground only to be evicted again. Grenades and automatic rifles were the most effective weapons of the Marine infantry in terrain well adapted to defense. At the bottom of this page the Marines are seen lying low while a barrage of white phosphorus hits the unseen enemy in the background. But some Japanese always weathered the storm.

This was the bomb! Not the identical A-bomb, of course, which gutted Hiroshima or Nagasaki in August, 1945. The explosion seen in this photograph took place in 1953 at Yucca Flat, Nevada. By that time the Marines were adjusting their tactics to the new weapon, and 2,100 participated in the Nevada maneuvers under the command of Brigadier General Wilburt C. Brown.

But in 1945, Americans had been stunned by President Truman's announcement: "That bomb had more power than twenty thousand tons of TNT . . . It is a harnessing of the basic power of the universe." And thus the war in the Pacific ended with a climax which meant that the tactics of World War II were obsolescent. A new era of war had dawned.

183

Simulated assault landings (above) from "Flying Banana" Piasecki HRP-1 helicopters were made at Quantico. The photograph below shows Marine Colonel Walter R. Walsh testing body armor by firing a .45-caliber submachine gun point-blank at a grim dummy.

KOREA

Tactics Created for Atomic Age

Never in history has there been a more somber victory than the triumph in the late summer of 1945, when Japan surrendered. Americans were too troubled by the responsibility for their new atomic weapon to take pride in its creation. The havoc it wrought in two Japanese cities was deplored rather than applauded, even though the island empire had reaped the whirlwind sown in the 1930's.

From a tactical viewpoint, moreover, "the bomb" was a mixed blessing. Although the dreadful secret was then believed to be solely in this nation's keeping, the new weapon rendered obsolescent American amphibious techniques, which had been the war's most effective tactical innovation.

The Marines realized that a single atomic blast could wipe out concentrations of ships and landing craft such as those seen at Saipan and Iwo Jima. Only tactical dispersion — dispersion on a scale never known before — could make possible an amphibious assault landing against an enemy using atomic weapons.

In 1946, General Alexander A. Vandegrift, then commandant, put it squarely up to the Marine Corps to find the tactical solution. Again, as in 1933, when the original amphibious tactics were worked out, Marine officers started from scratch at Quantico with nothing but a "prospective military philosophy," as it was described by Colonel Victor H. Krulak. "It consists of thinking in terms of the next war instead of the last. This means starting with ideas, when you have nothing more tangible, and developing them into the concepts, procedures and weapons of the future."

Only two dimensions of amphibious tactics — frontal and flank assault — had been available to Marine planners of 1933. But in 1946 the helicopter offered the possibility of a third dimension, as represented by vertical landings of troops from dispersed carriers.

Theory burgeoned into experiment in 1947, with the formation at Quantico of a Marine experimental helicopter squadron, HMX-1. Although no rotary-wing aircraft of that day could lift more than six men, in addition to the pilot, HMX-1 worked out techniques for the larger helicopters of the future.

Two Marine colonels, Merrill B. Twining and Edward C. Dyer, contributed much to the new doctrine of vertical assault landings. Meanwhile, at Camp Lejeune, N. C., a Navy Medical

FH-1 Phantom fighters, photographed in September, 1948, were the first jet planes of the Marines.

Service officer, Lieutenant Commander Frederick C. Lewis, was experimenting with lightweight Marine body armor, made possible by modern plastics.

OFF TO WAR AGAIN!

Seldom have Americans made greater sacrifices for their country than the Marine reservists of July, 1950. None of these civilians suspected that they would be called to combat duty only five years after the end of World War II. Many of them were veterans of that war who had married and started a family, and in some instances a new business suffered.

Parades and band music were conspicuously lacking when "the Minute Men of 1950" departed for Camp Pendleton on a few days' notice. It was business as usual for the country in general as tearful mothers, wives and sweethearts gathered at the railway or bus station for the leave-taking.

Events moved swiftly for the reservists. Only a month and a day after embarking with the 1st Marine Division, they were climbing the sea wall of an Asian port in one of history's greatest amphibious operations.

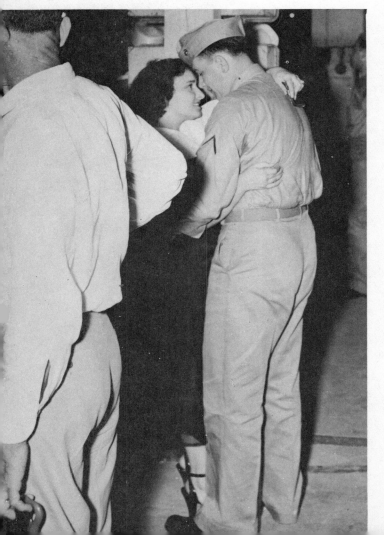

New Orleans is the scene of the photographs on this page, taken on the night when the reservists departed for combat duty in Korea.

The Minute Men of 1950

Americans had never given much thought to the 38th Parallel until the summer of 1950. It was vaguely remembered as a boundary set up in Korea between American and Russian occupation forces in August, 1945.

Before the war ended, our Russian allies had proved to be treacherous. Coming to the aid of the victors, they rushed into the political vacuum left in Manchuria and Korea to reap a prodigious harvest of loot. Nearly everything portable was seized, and thousands of Japanese prisoners were made slave laborers.

The 38th Parallel divides the Korean peninsula roughly into halves. In the north the Russians created a puppet state and trained an army of 100,000 North Koreans for aggression. On June 25, 1950, these Korean Reds crossed the 38th Parallel with tanks and planes to invade the Republic of Korea. Not only did they overwhelm the lightly armed forces of the Republic; they also defeated the first outnumbered U. S. troops after the United Nations decided on armed intervention.

Then, belatedly, Americans realized how much the national defenses had been neglected in the five years since the peak of our military might. Only occupation troops from Japan were available at first, but on July 7, 1950, the 1st Provisional Marine Brigade was activated. Five days later it embarked from San Diego under the command of Brigadier General Edward A. Craig — an infantry regiment and air group numbering 6,534 men.

These were "the Minute Men of 1950" — the Marine reservists who made it possible to recruit units of career Marines up to war strength. By bus, train and plane they poured into Camp Pendleton in California, until, on August 14, Major General Oliver P. Smith's 1st Marine Division was ready to embark for Korea, where it would absorb the Brigade.

Thus did the Marine Corps fulfill its mission as "a Force in Readiness."

Marine machine gunners are shown (below) as they boarded ship to serve with the Brigade in Korea.

Temperatures above a hundred during the first action of the Brigade in Korea caused prostration from heat exhaustion. Marine helicopters and observation planes dropped cans of water to the assault troops.

Obong-ni Ridge in the photograph above is the hill to the left in the background. Twice the Marines attacked in this area when the Korean Reds crossed the Naktong River to threaten the line of communications.

Marines Are "Firemen" of the Pusan Perimeter

The first Marines to land in Korea disembarked at Pusan on August 2, 1950. A perimeter around that supply port was held by the hard-pressed U. S. Army and South Korean troops, who had been compelled to give ground before Korean Red material superiority throughout July.

The American public, dazed by this result, had begun to realize that the country had a war on its hands, not a "police action." (It was still not considered proper, however, to call it a war.) Newspaper readers and radio listeners had to learn several new sets of initials:

EUSAK — Eighth U. S. Army in Korea
ROK — Republic of Korea
NKPA — North Korean People's Army

Lieutenant General Walton H. Walker, commanding general of EUSAK, decided to use the Marine brigade aircraft group as a mobile reserve — "firemen" to put out a tactical blaze at any part of the thinly held UN line. A few days after landing, they were rushed to the southern coast to block an "end run" by NKPA columns, which

suffered their first sustained reverse since their original aggression.

Twice more during the month, the Marines of the Brigade fought alongside EUSAK units. Both times they attacked in the Obong-ni Ridge area to hurl back Korean Reds, who had crossed the Naktong to threaten the Pusan lifeline.

The combat helicopter (above) had its historical debut in Korea, but the faithful old Corsair (right) was the workhorse of the Marines.

The sea wall at Inchon was one of the greatest tactical obstacles as the Marines attacked on the murky and overcast late afternoon of September 15, 1950. The assault troops are seen with scaling ladders in the photograph above, as their landing craft head for Inchon, a dim haze in the distance. In the lower photograph the attackers are swarming over the wall on Red Beach, to fight in the streets and alleys. Although the North Korean radio had warned of the possibility of the attack as early as the 13th, the enemy had not made adequate preparations to defend the city.

Inchon or Bust!

The first and only amphibious assault of the Korean conflict was the concept of General Douglas MacArthur, commander-in-chief of UN forces.

No ship-to-shore assault ever faced more hazardous difficulties. High tides, mud flats and tortuous channels made the harbor a planner's nightmare. Only a few days each month could be used because of these handicaps, so that the element of surprise was lost.

Moreover, a fortified harbor island, Wolmi-do, must be secured before the assault on Inchon, so that the landing craft would not be exposed to flanking fire. This meant that Wolmi-do must be taken on the morning high tide, giving Inchon a whole day to prepare for a late afternoon attack.

Only two infantry regiments of Major General Oliver P. Smith's 1st Marine Division had arrived for D day, so little time had been available for embarkation. But thanks to Navy and Marine amphibious know-how, the attack of Sept. 15, 1950, succeeded beyond expectation.

There were, of course, some anxious moments. In order to have supplies immediately available, eight LSTs were beached on the Inchon water front shortly after the troops landed. A few enemy mortar shells hit ships loaded with gasoline, but by a miracle no blaze resulted.

Inchon was largely secured by midnight, and supplies were landed for the next day. The operation, which might have been another Tarawa, had cost the Marines a total of 17 killed, 2 missing, 165 wounded. Enemy casualties were estimated at 1,650, including 300 prisoners.

"**Mopping up**" **on Wolmi-do,** as seen in the photograph above, was completed before noon on the morning of the attack. General MacArthur sent a message of congratulation from his flagship, the *Mount McKinley:* "The Navy and Marines have never shone more brightly than this morning." The photograph below shows two of six Russian T-34 tanks knocked out by the Marines on Sept. 17, 1950, as they advanced to Kimpo Airfield.

Amphibian trucks and tractors were the Marine vehicles for an assault crossing of the broad, tidal Han River on September 20, 1950. Kimpo Airfield, largest in Korea, had been secured on the 18th, along with the prisoners shown in the photograph at the left. They don't look like very formidable adversaries, squatting forlornly with an ROK soldier on guard in the background. But the Marines found them worthy opponents on occasion. On the opposite page a Marine is seen raising the flag over the American consulate in Seoul while the street fighting is still raging. And below the Marines are examining captured 120mm mortars in a Seoul schoolyard.

THE FIGHT FOR SEOUL

Three Marine infantry regiments — the third one having arrived a week after the Inchon landing — had the task of capturing an Oriental city with a 1,500,000 prewar population.

The enemy put up a last-ditch fight in the hills northwest of the city. One Marine company had all its officers killed or wounded save one, and only 26 enlisted men were left unhurt. But the assault troops had taken a position defended by an NKPA battalion.

The fight in the streets of Seoul went on, night and day, for 48 hours. Another NKPA battalion, supported by Russian-built T-34 tanks, made a night attack down a main boulevard, only to be annihilated. By September 27, 1950, the city was largely secured, though isolated groups continued to resist. The Marine division, as part of Major General Edward M. Almond's X Corps, advanced through the heart of Seoul while troops of the 7th Infantry Division cleared the enemy from the northeastern outskirts.

The Marines Had a Name
for It: Operation Yo-Yo

Early in October, 1950, there could be no doubt that the NKPA was on its last legs. The Inchon-Seoul operation of X Corps had been the strategic anvil, and the northward drive of EUSAK the hammer. When they met, during the last days of September, there was nothing left for the Korean Reds but flight. Thousands of them avoided capture by wearing civilian garments.

General MacArthur decided to send the Marines by sea to the east coast for an assault landing at Wonsan to cut off that escape route. Other X Corps units were to follow. Meanwhile, the Eighth Army would advance along the west coast to take the NKPA capital, Pyongyang.

Those who have never seen the embarkation

of a division cannot imagine the prodigious amount of gear that must be taken. But the Marines at last embarked from Inchon and rounded the peninsula, only to sail monotonously back and forth, twelve hours in each direction, for a week. The reason for this odd performance was that the invasion fleet had to wait for mine clearance in Wonsan Harbor. The Marines named it Operation Yo-Yo. Adding to their disgust, Wonsan had already been occupied without a fight by ROK troops.

"Home by Christmas!" was heard everywhere. A possibility of Red China's intervening was mentioned, but nobody put much stock in it as the Marines made a tame administrative landing.

Marines who landed at Wonsan on October 26, 1950, could not have supposed that they would have much use for the tanks being disgorged from the capacious mouths of the LSTs. Nor could they have imagined what a hostile terrain awaited them, as shown in the aerial photograph on the opposite page. "A cliff on one side and a chasm on the other" was an apt description of the twisting road leading from Hungnam to the Chosin Reservoir — a road that the Marines were to know too well in coming weeks. For the Chinese Communist Forces (CCF) had already crossed the Yalu and were secretly massing in North Korea. In a few more weeks the blow would fall and the Marines would be battling for life in sub-zero weather.

The desolate landscape seen by Marines advancing from Hungnam and Hamhung to the Chosin Reservoir, is shown in the photograph above. The troops had their first fight with the new enemy on November 4-7, 1950, when a Marine regiment got the better of a Chinese division. Then the enemy mysteriously disappeared, and the Marines occupied Hagaru„ at the foot of the Reservoir, without any trouble. This town was made the advance CP of the 1st Marine Division, which maintained its headquarters at Hamhung as other X Corps units followed. CCF prisoners were warmly clad in padded cotton uniforms, as seen in the photograph to the left, but wore tennis shoes and had no mittens. Apparently they had expected to win a quick victory.

Frozen Chosin

Not only did the landscape in northeast Korea look desolate; it actually was the wildest part of a peninsula where every foot of fertile soil is tilled. Siberian tigers were once found in these hills and bears are still hunted.

This fact was demonstrated to a Marine one night when a bear tried to share his foxhole. It is a matter of record that both Marine and bear withdrew hastily. But the Marine tale that the animal was wearing a hammer-and-sickle emblem may be doubted.

General MacArthur ordered an advance of X Corps to the Yalu in northeast Korea while the Eighth Army swept up the west coast. He believed that these drives would end NKPA resistance and regarded CCF intervention as improbable in spite of the fights of Marine and EUSAK units with the Chinese several weeks before.

On November 25, 1950, he launched his "massive compression envelopment" with EUSAK advancing in West Korea and X Corps attacking on the 27th as the other arm of the pincers. But the enemy had different ideas. And his counteroffensive dealt U. S. forces one of the greatest defeats ever suffered by American arms.

Chinese dead, on the outskirts of Yudam-ni, are shown in the photograph above, and below are CCF prisoners in the act of surrendering to a Marine foot patrol.

The Advance to the Rear

When X Corps attacked west of the Chosin Reservoir on November 27, 1950, the Eighth Army offensive had already been stopped cold by a surprise CCF counteroffensive. These UN troops were separated from X Corps by 80 miles, so that mutual support was out of the question.

Against negligible opposition, the Marines advanced two miles from Yudam-ni, on a western arm of the Reservoir. Shortly before midnight, they were beset by Chinese Reds in overwhelming numbers. The Marine battalion at Hagaru was attacked on the 28th, and air reconnaissance reported that the 70-mile supply route from Hamhung to Yudam-ni had been cut in five places.

In other words, the 1st Marine Division had been sliced into five morsels for the tactical mastication of eight CCF divisions, numbering at least 60,000 men. This was the beginning of one of the great epics of American military annals, as the Marines fought their way to the seacoast in their "advance to the rear." It took thirteen sub-zero days of hard fighting and cost the Marines nearly 4,000 killed and wounded, in addition to 7,000 non-battle casualties, chiefly frostbite cases.

Close air support during every daylight hour was always needed by the Marines who fought their way to safety in the Chosin Reservoir breakout. On the opposite page are two views of a F4U-5 Corsair blasting the enemy just ahead of the Marine advance. In the lower photograph the plane can barely be seen in the cloud of flame and smoke billowing up from the explosion. On this page are three views of the Marine infantry patrols, beating off Chinese Reds who tried to attack the flanks of the vehicle column.

THE 13-DAY BATTLE

It was a 13-day battle, with few interludes, that the Marines fought over the first half of the 70-mile route. The rest of the way was free from opposition.

Half a mile an hour was considered a good pace in view of the fights to clear the flanks. In fact, it took the Marines at Yudam-ni three days to cover the 14 miles to Hagaru.

That town at the foot of the Chosin Reservoir was the assembly area for the Marines and three Army battalions. There they evacuated more than 3,000 wounded men in C-47s from an airstrip hastily hacked out of the frozen earth. General Almond, commanding X Corps, offered to fly out all the troops in an aerial Dunkirk after the destruction of weapons. But General Smith insisted on a fighting breakout.

When a vital bridge was destroyed, C-119s flew in sections of a Treadway bridge that was the salvation of Marine vehicles.

XENOPHON DID IT

The breakout of the Marines recalled the march of Xenophon and the immortal Ten Thousand as the Greeks cut their way through Asiatic hordes to the sea in 401 B.C. Twenty-three centuries later the U. S. Marines used much the same tactics, allowing for differences in weapons.

In both instances it was found essential to set up virtually a mobile 360° perimeter, with the vehicles protected by infantry from front, flank or rear attacks. Only the severely wounded Marines rode, some of them so helpless that they had to be strapped to the seats and covered with blankets. The walking wounded trudged alongside the trucks with rifles and added to Marine firepower.

Five views of the Marine breakout are shown on these pages. As the long vehicle column ground to a halt while the infantry cleared the flanks up ahead, the parka-clad Marines — many of them walking wounded—sagged to the roadside in utter exhaustion. They had snatched only a few fitful hours of sleep in any one of the thirteen nights. They had eaten only a few warm meals in thirteen days while subsisting for the most part on frozen "C" rations. Yet they staggered to their feet when the column moved again and resumed the march, often enough on frostbitten feet. Never in any past war of our history have Americans shown greater courage and endurance than the "Reservoir Marines."

Amphibious Operation in Reverse

The defeat suffered by the Eighth Army was one of the worst of American history. Northwest Korea was given up in the subsequent retreat. This left X Corps isolated and General MacArthur ordered a redeployment to South Korea.

Called an "amphibious operation in reverse," the gigantic lift by sea was perhaps the greatest accomplishment of the Navy in the Korean war. In two weeks, 105,000 U. S. and ROK troops were embarked, along with 91,000 Korean civilian refugees, 17,500 vehicles and 350,000 tons of cargo. All this without the loss of a single man to enemy action!

It was believed that the remnants of eight CCF divisions were capable of attacking. But later it was learned that they needed three months to reorganize and get back into action, so severely had they been punished by the Marines. Thus the remaining X Corps troops had no trouble while awaiting their turn, after the battered Marine division had embarked. Naval gunfire sufficed to keep the enemy at a respectful distance as the last troops departed.

Landing craft were taking Marines from the beach to the ships this time. One of them found time for a hot bath while he was waiting.

GIVEN UP FOR LOST

The Marines were astonished, upon completing their breakout, to learn that they had been virtually given up for lost by the American public. Newspaper headlines told of the Marine "encirclement," and editorials warned that a wholesale slaughter or surrender might be the outcome.

The entire nation responded with prayerful gratitude to the news that the Marines were coming out fighting, with all their arms and gear. Ever since the reverses during the early weeks of the Korean war, commentators had been lamenting the supposed physical decline of young American manhood. But American pride was redeemed by the breakout from the Chosin Reservoir. The Marines had more than held their own with tough Chinese peasants when it came to enduring hardships.

Mountains of cargo were loaded on ships commanded by Rear Admiral James H. Doyle in a redeployment completed on Christmas Eve.

Marine infantry advancing in Operation Ripper had the support of their own artillery, directed by air observation. Snow was still on the ground as torrential rains slowed up Marines plodding to the attack across rice paddies, such as the troops seen above. But the men usually took their objective.

Chinese Hard Hit in Spring of 1951

One Eighth Army offensive after another hit the Chinese Reds in the spring of 1951, keeping them off balance as they prepared for their "Fifth Phase Offensive." This drive, they boasted, would bring the war to a victorious end.

The year had begun badly for UN forces when the Communists followed up their victories in November with a great offensive which exploded on New Year's Eve. Lieutenant General Matthew B. Ridgway had just arrived to take command after the death of General Walker in a jeep accident. He put up the best defense he could with an army not yet recovered from its reverses, but it was necessary to evacuate Seoul.

Ridgway seized the initiative in February when he launched Operation Killer. His purpose was "the destruction of enemy soldiers, not the acquisition of Korean real estate."

Operation Ripper followed on the heels of the first offensive, taking the Eighth Army past the 38th Parallel. At last the Communists were goaded into striking back prematurely, and their offensive was launched on April 22, 1951. The enemy broke through in the area of an ROK division on the left of the 1st Marine Division. The Marines had to fight off enemies in front and on the flank for two nights, but they kept their lines intact.

The Chinese made only a few gains, and suffered terrible casualties, as Eighth Army units fell back to prepared positions. On May 16, following a lull, the Chinese tried again. And again they were horribly punished by the UN forces in effective counterattacks.

It was evident by this time that the Eighth Army was one of the finest military instruments of American history and certainly the most cosmopolitan. Units ranging from company to battalion strength represented Australia, Belgium, Canada, France, Greece, Luxembourg, the Netherlands, New Zealand, the Philippines, Thailand, Turkey and the United Kingdom.

Weapon teams and small patrols did much of the fighting in the first war of the new Atomic Age, as the photographs on this page indicate.

Red China Near Knockout, Needs Interval for Recovery

When Red China's offensive sputtered out like a damp firecracker in May, 1951, the Eighth Army launched a counterstroke which soon had the enemy in trouble. Lieutenant General James A. Van Fleet, who relieved Ridgway in April after that general took MacArthur's place, was certain that the Chinese were defeated.

"In June, 1951, we had them whipped," commented the new Eighth Army commander. "They were definitely gone. They were in awful shape."

It is an old Communist trick to pretend an interest in peace for the purpose of gaining a breathing spell. Americans might have recalled in 1951 that the Reds had taken advantage of truce negotiations for military gains in China when prospects for a Nationalist victory were bright. While prolonging the talks, in 1945, the Communists had profited by reorganizing their armies.

History repeated itself late in June, 1951, when the Reds took the initiative in proposing truce talks. They made it appear by trickery that the United Nations were begging for terms. UN delegates to the Kaesong conference were requested to put white flags on cars for identification. But Chinese photographs made it appear that they came as losers seeking an armistice. This propaganda convinced millions of illiterate Asians.

Actually, the CCF armies were in a desperate situation when saved by the lull. Ten thousand soldiers surrendered to the advancing Eighth Army in a single June week as remnants of Chinese companies threw away their weapons and gave up in a body. It could hardly be believed that these had been the fanatics of 1950, when Chinese soldiers frequently died fighting rather than surrender.

The Marines, now a part of X Corps again, could testify to the slaughter of enemy units seeking to escape the pounding they were taking from UN artillery. It was not an uncommon sight to see several hundred Chinese bodies awaiting a mass burial while a 'dozer scooped out a common grave.

No longer could the Communists win by human tonnage and a ruthless sacrifice of men that would never be tolerated in a democratic nation. They were definitely beaten in June, 1951.

Close air support for the advancing Marines in Operation Killer is seen in this photograph of a Corsair bombing a Chinese strong point in east-central Korea. Two Marine infantrymen with a radio are lying low in the foreground.

The combat photographs on this page were taken late in May, 1951, when the Eighth Army counterattacks had the Chinese staggering. At the top are shown enemy bodies awaiting burial after the Marines repulsed a CCF night attack. The middle photograph is of Marine tanks in pursuit of retreating Chinese Reds. And below is a view of a Marine white phosphorus shell bursting in front of a machine-gun position. Horrible burns resulted from these shells.

Marine transport helicopters, as seen on this page, were equally well adapted to troop movements from a carrier or from the frozen mountains of Korea. On the opposite page is another carrier photograph, and below it a Marine signals to the pilot of an HRS-1 picking up a cargo net full of ammunition.

The Choppers

The helicopter has a good claim to being the foremost tactical innovation of Korea, and the Marine Corps an equally good claim to taking the lead in its development.

The first helicopter squadron in Korea was Marine Observation Squadron 6 (VMO-6), which arrived in August, 1950. Composed half of three-place Sikorsky helicopters and half of OY observation planes, VMO-6 found the "choppers" useful for casualty evacuation, wire-laying and rescue missions. For command purposes they were the general's steed of the twentieth century, restoring a front-line leadership threatened with extinction.

In September, 1951, when Marine Helicopter Squadron 161 (HMR-161) reached Korea, greater possibilities were realized. Lifts of a battalion of combat-equipped troops to a mountaintop became a commonplace. The Marine transport helicopter, the HRS-1, could fly four to six combat-equipped men or a payload of 1,420 pounds at sea level. Rocket launchers or 75mm pack howitzers could be picked up with their crews. As a grand climax, HMR-161 supplied two regiments at the front for five days. A total of 1,612,306 pounds of cargo was lifted by an average of 12 aircraft over a distance of 8 miles.

Wounded Man's Chances of Survival 200 to 1

Five years had given the lessons of World War II time to be assimilated, so that Korea represented an advance in military surgery. Credit is also due to the first large-scale use of helicopters for casualty evacuation.

During the three weeks of the Inchon-Seoul operation, the 1st Medical Battalion of the 1st Marine Division treated 2,484 surgical patients. Nine died after reaching the operating room, six of them following major surgery. The proportion of patients surviving was about 99.6 per cent.

Casualty evacuation in Korea is pictured on the opposite page as comrades bring a wounded Marine to a Bell HLT-4 helicopter for a flight to a rear-area medical aid station. In twenty minutes he will have definitive surgery.

This meant that a man's chances of coming out alive were 200 to 1, provided he could last long enough to reach the operating table.

His prospects of speedy evacuation were improved by the helicopter. Whereas in the past — meaning the World War II era, which seemed remote to youngsters fighting in Korea — it had often taken five hours to carry a patient in a litter from the firing line to an ambulance, the helicopter needed only minutes to fly a man from the front to a base hospital.

Modern body armor, made of lightweight plastics and worn by Marine and Army combat troops in the last half of the Korean war, further reduced fatalities. It would be a conservative estimate to say that this protection doubled a man's chances, as compared to the earlier months of the conflict. It reduced serious wounds to light and prevented light wounds altogether.

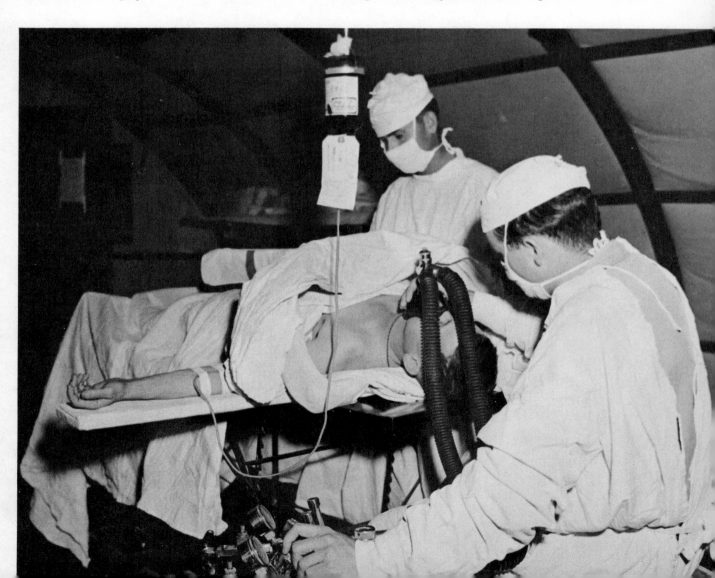

KOREA'S WESTERN FRONT

The Korean war and a change of character after the lulls due to the truce talks in the summer and fall of 1951. A warfare of movement turned into static warfare, reminiscent of the Western Front in 1916.

The lulls enabled the Chinese to bring up as much artillery as the UN forces. They dug defenses in depth which could only have been taken at a prohibitive cost in casualties.

Opposing lines of trenches scarred the Korean peninsula from sea to sea as the war went underground. Prefabricated bunkers were flown to the Eighth Army by helicopters, and regimental command posts were wired for electricity. Probably never in history did troops eat so well, yet it was dangerous duty. Patrols at night ran the risk of being surprised with burp guns and grenades at ten feet, and Americans were at a disadvantage against Chinese, accustomed to the dark all their lives.

Marines of an outpost, waiting to be relieved, are shown on the opposite page the morning after beating off a predawn Chinese attack. Seen in the lower photograph is the S-3 (operations) bunker of a Marine artillery battalion. Note the electric light hanging over the plotting table. During the last sixteen months of the war the Marines were a part of I Corps, holding a sector athwart the historic invasion route of west Korea. On this page is shown one of the sleek, twin-engine F2H-2P "Banshee" jet fighters, equipped for photography. And in the lower picture is an aerial view of Eighth Army trenches.

By day the front could be deceptively tranquil, but you never dared relax after dark.

Ready-to-Wear Foxholes

The Knights of old doubtless would have been astonished to see the armor of 1952 — those lightweight (eight and a half pounds) combat vests made of 12-ply, basketweave nylon and ⅛-inch slabs of glass cloth filaments, bonded together under heavy pressure.

But there was no question about the effectiveness of the protection that all U. S. combat troops had before the end of the war in Korea. Wounds that might have been fatal or serious became light wounds, and light wounds bad bruises. The over-all reduction in U. S. casualties was estimated all the way from 50 to 70 per cent and more. Morale and combat effectiveness invariably showed a gain after the vests were issued.

Body armor saved the life of this Marine, who escaped with a bruise instead of a very serious wound.

Troop acceptance was enthusiastic. Some of the Marines scoffed at the "bullet-proof" vest until they saw for themselves that it could save lives. Then it became standard equipment at the front.

Modern body armor is no better than paper against rifle or machine-gun fire. But it can stop most grenade, mortar and artillery fragments as well as bullets from submachine guns, pistols and other low-velocity firearms.

The Marine Corps took the lead in development, and 63,000 vests were supplied to the Army, which issued a vest of its own toward the end of the war. Troop acceptance was enthusiastic in both services as men proudly showed the hole in the vest and the ugly contusion — the only proof of the impact of a murderous shell fragment. On the basis of Korean experience, there is no doubt that modern body armor is here to stay.

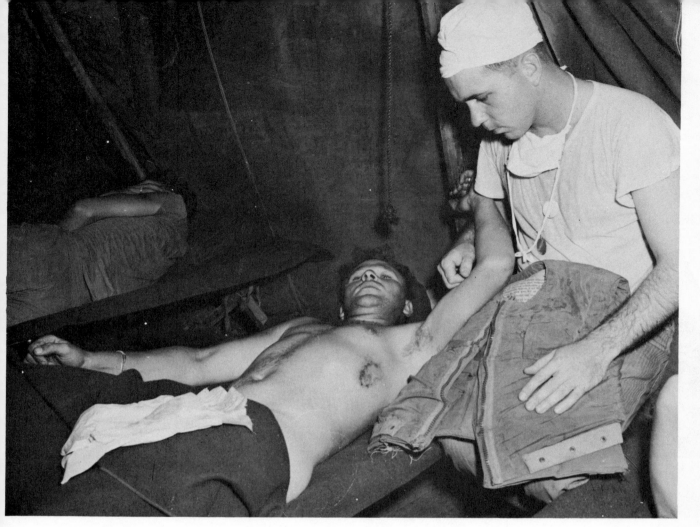

A painful bruise that might have been a fatal penetration to the heart is shown above. A Navy surgeon holds the Marine private's armored vest. Below are pictured Lieutenant Commander Frederick J. Lewis, of the Navy Medical Service, and Marine wounded men examining a vest that gave protection.

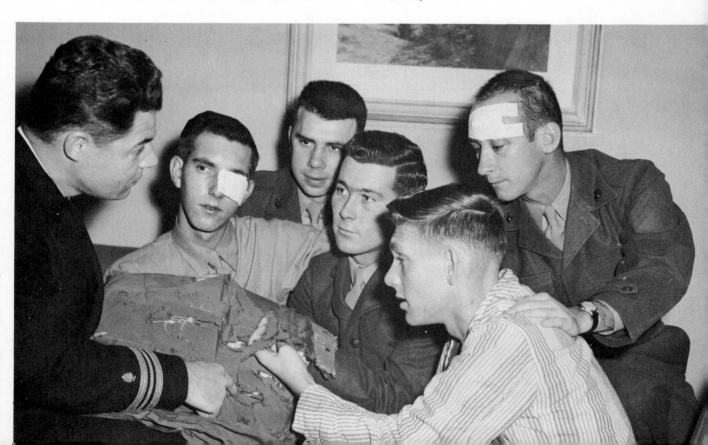

Korean War Ends in a Stalemate

The UN forces could have breached the CCF lines during the long period of static warfare in Korea. But it would have been an empty triumph purchased at an exorbitant cost in casualties. And if the Chinese had been evicted from Korea, the United Nations would have faced the problem of whether to invade Manchuria at the risk of bringing on World War III.

Hence the Korean conflict ended in a stalemate with the cease-fire of July 27, 1953. The most unpopular war ever waged by the United States since the War of 1812, it was not fought in vain. The challenge of Communism had been met on an ideal battleground from the American viewpoint — a theater of operations far removed from U. S. soil, yet vulnerable to air and naval superiority and within a few hours of bases in Japan.

Finally, Korea served as a warning that the nation dared not risk disaster by neglecting its defenses as it had during the five years after World War II. Our preliminary defeats in Korea aroused us from complacency to a realistic appraisal of the dangers we faced.

The leopard's spots might have inspired the battle dress of this Marine lieutenant returning from a patrol, and below is a grim-faced machine-gun crew.

The face of death may be seen in the two photographs on this page without risk or discomfort. Pictured above is the explosion of an enemy 82mm mortar shell, and below is a view of the demolition of Chinese bunkers with grenades and planted charges, just ahead of an advancing Marine. Mortar and artillery shells were the principal cause of casualties in the outpost warfare of opposing forces taking to cover in bunkers and trenches. Although the Eighth Army had the advantage of aerial observation and spotting, Chinese artillery was amazingly accurate. And CCF intelligence was so good that incoming U. S. outfits were "welcomed" by loudspeaker with their correct unit designations.

"Eighth and Eye" in the vocabulary of the Marines means the residence of the commandant at Eighth and I Streets, S. E., Washington, D. C. — the oldest continu- ously occupied public building in the city. Shown above is a sunset parade, with the famous old landmark seen in the background of the photograph.

SEMPER FIDELIS

Just as Eighth and Eye is the social center of the Marine Corps, the Navy Arlington Annex is the administrative center. The photograph above was taken at 4:30 P.M., quitting time for 10,000 Civil Service employees and Navy or Marine "personnel," as they are known in their own triplicate documents.

The Annex, across the Potomac from Washington, sits upon a hill overlooking the Pentagon, less than half a mile away. Originally a three-story warehouse of World War II, it became a makeshift office building with the addition of a fourth floor. Only three elevators serve the rambling structure, and freight has precedence over passengers. Marine Corps Headquarters, with the

offices of the commandant and other high-ranking officers, shares the Annex with several Navy bureaus.

Visitors are always astonished at the spectacle of offices in which colonels almost literally rub elbows with corporals and Civil Service typists. Space is at a premium and therefore only the narrowest of aisles are left between phalanxes of desks.

Semper Fidelis is the motto of the Corps, and the Marines are always faithful to the coffee percolator that is standard equipment for every office. The working day begins at eight with a cup for the colonel, and he will require several refills before noon.

219

Quantico

The nearest approach to a Marine West Point or Annapolis is found at Quantico, Va., a 30-mile drive from Washington, D. C. Nearly all the officer-students at the Marine base have graduated from some college or university. At Quantico they take courses in military subjects. Usually they report for a two-year tour of duty, and it is not uncommon for an officer to be an instructor in one course and a student in another.

Shown in the photographs on this page are Breckinridge Hall (left) and Ellis Hall (below), a new building named in memory of Lieutenant Colonel Earl H. Ellis, the brilliant Marine officer whose life ended mysteriously on a Japanese-mandated island of the Pacific in 1923.

Although tactics of armed destruction are taught in these halls, they have the peaceful atmosphere of a campus. Not even the ivy and co-eds are lacking, for courses are also given to officers of the Women Marines.

Little Hall, shown in the photograph above, is the central meeting place of the military community. In this building are the post exchange, the theater and the "hostess house," where visitors are entertained.

The mess hall of an enlisted men's barracks at Quantico is seen below. So appetizing and plentiful is the food that veteran sergeants with desk jobs have to fight the Battle of the Bulge three times a day.

Woman Marines

The Marinettes of World War I were a distant memory when the Women Marines of the second World War came into being on February 1, 1943, nearly a year after the formation of women's services in the U. S. Army and Navy.

No such name as WAC, WAVE or SPAR was ever contemplated. It was believed that the simple designation Women Marines would give more of a feeling of belonging to the Corps. The informal abbreviation WR (Women's Reserve) is often heard, too.

"Free a man to fight" was the slogan in World War II, and it is estimated that the WRs managed to replace nearly the equivalent of a combat division.

The approximate strength of the Women Marines in the summer of 1958 was 120 officers and 1,500 enlisted. A total of 154 officers and 3,609 enlisted served at various periods during the Korean War.

WRs marching in winter uniforms (left) and in well-pressed fatigues (below) are seen on this page. Opposite are WRs in summer uniforms at Parris Island (upper), and the lower photograph shows Private Patricia Hamilton being taught new duties at the Cherry Point, N. C., air base by Sergeant Charles M. Higgins.

No menial duties are required of Women Marines. Assignments range from typist, clerk and bookkeeper to such specialties as radar technician, air traffic controller and data processor.

The fondness of the WRs for marching and drill is the wonder of male colleagues. But their femininity is never submerged, and formal dresses are worn more often than uniforms on weekend evenings.

MARINE INSTITUTE GIVES 132 COURSES

More than half a million Marine officers and men — 588,293, to be exact — have taken Marine Corps Institute courses at nominal cost during its first 38 years. And the 13 subjects offered in 1920 have grown to 132 in 1958.

"This school is a revolution," said Brigadier General Smedley D. ("Old Gimlet Eye") Butler shortly after its foundation. "It is something new. The old officers of the Marine Corps would turn over in their graves if they knew what we were doing, because in the old days they did nothing but soldier. We want to make . . . the whole Marine Corps a great university."

From the beginning the Institute has been associated with the International Correspondence Schools. A student completing a course receives a certificate from the Schools as well as the Marine Corps.

Pfc Don E. Corbett (left) is shown taking an examination, and (below) Marine instructors are being given a refresher course in an engineering subject.

MCI instructors are seen filing out of one of the Institute's buildings in Washington. They are required to undergo constant training. MCI courses include many cultural as well as military subjects.

Marine Corps Band Is "National Band"

"The Marine Band is eminently the national band of the country; it has been so closely identified with the interests of the Capital that it has been known for years as 'the President's Band.'"

So said the Washington *Evening Star* of September 2, 1873, when announcing the appointment of Louis Schneider as leader. Seven years later, John Philip Sousa replaced Schneider as the most famous leader of a band whose history may be traced back to the fifes and drums of the Continental Marines in 1775.

On a June day in 1886 the Marine Band played Mendelssohn's *Wedding March* when President Grover Cleveland and Frances Folsom were married in the White House. Long afterwards the "March King" proudly recalled the mathematical precision with which he timed the descent of the musicians down the steps of the executive mansion.

Sousa completed and copyrighted his march *Semper Fidelis* in 1888, naming it after the Marine motto. The Marine Band went on a nation-wide concert tour three years later. Instruments consisted of 14 B clarinets, 2 alto clarinets, 4 French horns, 4 saxophones, 2 flutes, 2 oboes, 2

John Philip Sousa, the "March King," is shown in the photograph above; and below is pictured the Marine Band in the 1880's, with only one smooth-shaven man seen.

bassoons, 4 cornets, 2 trumpets, 2 fleugel horns and 3 trombones. Drums are not mentioned in this list, but it may be assumed that they were included.

Sousa was succeeded by Francisco Fanciulli in 1892, and six years later William H. Santelman became leader until 1927 — a period of 29 years. His son, William F. H. Santelman, took over in 1940, replacing Taylor Branson.

The musical library of the Marine Band is one of the greatest in the world. Stored at the Marine Barracks in Washington are more than 12,000 compositions, among them 2,000 marches. The collection is valued at two million dollars. It includes rare compositions not found in any other musical library, some of them dating back to the eighteenth century.

The Marine Band giving a concert on the grounds of the U. S. Capitol toward the end of World War II is shown in the photograph above. Below is a portrait of William F. H. Santelman, leader of the Marine Band since 1940.

The commandant is the only Marine general holding four-star rank. He is entitled to sit in on the deliberations of the Joint Chiefs of Staff and to vote on issues concerning the Marine Corps. Above, left to right, are pictured Commandants Thomas Holcomb, Alexander A. Vandegrift and Clifton B. Cates. Holcomb, who commanded a Marine infantry battalion in Belleau Wood, directed Marine amphibious training and preparations for World War II during his long term from 1936 to 1943. Vandegrift, 1944-1947, was the Marine commander on Guadalcanal when Japanese land forces were stopped for the first time. Cates, a lieutenant in Belleau Wood, was commandant during the critical first months of the war in Korea. Below is a photograph of the main entrance of the commandant's residence in Washington, D. C. Through these venerable portals have passed some of the most famous figures of American history.

Lemuel C. Shepherd, Jr. and Randolph McCall Pate (left to right) were the twentieth and twenty-first commandants. Shepherd, 1952-1956, another Belleau Wood veteran, was a Marine division commander on Okinawa. Pate, a lieutenant colonel on Guadalcanal, commanded a Marine division in Korea as the war ended. He was made commandant in January, 1956. Below is a photograph of the commandant's residence at sunset, with the last rays reflected by the windows.

Senator Paul H. Douglas (above), of Illinois, holds the record as the oldest man ever to go through Marine boot camp training. Volunteering in 1942 at the age of 50, he was twice wounded in Pacific island campaigns and ended five years of active duty as a lieutenant colonel in the USMC Reserve. Senator Douglas was a member of the faculty of the University of Chicago prior to his enlistment and had been a Chicago alderman. He was decorated with a Bronze Star Medal for heroism.

Senator George A. Smathers, of Florida, is shown above as a Marine captain at the head of his company as it marched to entrain from a North Carolina camp to San Diego in 1942 for overseas duty. At the left is Representative Donald J. Jackson, of California, a major in the Marine Reserve with a record of nine years of service, four of them in World War II. This photograph was taken in 1955 when he visited a Marine camp in Japan.

12 FORMER MARINES
IN 84th CONGRESS

Three Senators and nine Representatives of the 84th Congress were former Marines. Following is the list:

SENATE — Paul H. Douglas (D), Ill.; Michael J. Mansfield (D), Mont.; George A. Smathers (D), Fla.

HOUSE OF REPRESENTATIVES — Jack B. Brooks (D), Tex.; Paul B. Dague (R), Pa.; James C. Davis (D), Ga.; James P. S. Devereaux (R), Md.; Joe Holt (R), Calif.; Donald J. Jackson (R), Calif.; James Roosevelt (D), Calif.; Clark W. Thompson (D), Tex.; William M. Tuck (D), Va.

World War I was represented by four Congressmen, World War II by eight, and one legislator served in both World War II and the Korean conflict. The twelve men had a total of 64 years of service, consisting largely of combat duty. With the exception of Devereaux, the hero of Wake Island, who put in 25 years as a career Marine, all of the Congressmen were wartime volunteers.

Jack B. Brooks (above left) a Texas Representative, saw two years of combat duty in the Pacific. Representative Paul B. Dague, of Pennsylvania, a 1918 Marine, is shown greeting Marine Corporal Dora Schlitzkus.

Odyssey of a Marine Officer

There is no such thing as a typical Marine officer. But Major William T. Hickman is at least representative of a group who were too young for World War II. These Marines saw their first action as lieutenants in Korea.

Bill Hickman's story begins on a March day in 1943, two months after his seventeenth birthday. From his home town of Haddonfield, N. J., he rode ten miles on his bicycle to Philadelphia and enlisted. Because of his good scholastic and athletic record, he was selected as officer material.

As a Marine private he reported after high school graduation in June to Princeton University for three semesters. Next came engineering courses at Yale, where Bill won another football letter to add to his Princeton letter.

Early in 1945 he took boot-camp training at Parris Island. V-J Day found him in the Platoon Commander's School at Quantico. He could have gone home as a civilian with no strings attached, but Bill chose a Marine officer's career. He was one of 41 candidates to graduate from Basic School at Quantico as second lieutenants in April, 1946. Following are his assignments of the next twelve years:

1946-1948 — infantry duty in China.

1949-1950 — artillery school at Fort Sill, Okla.; artillery duty at Camp Lejeune.

1951 — the Mediterranean cruise with the Sixth Fleet.

1951-1952 — front-line duty in Korea as air observer and artillery battery commander.

1953-1955 — instructor at Army artillery school at Fort Sill.

1956-1959 — historian of Korean operations at Marine Headquarters, Washington, D. C.

Bill did not find promotion merely a matter of seniority. Of the 41 officers who graduated in his class at Basic School, only 21 survived with him to a major's rank in 1957. Casualties or resignations accounted for five, and 14 had their careers ended or retarded when selection boards found them wanting.

Private Hickman is seen above as a 17-year-old freshman at Princeton. At the right is a snapshot, taken nine years later, of Captain Hickman as an artillery battery commander in Korea. He had recently been an air observer, with 400 flight hours to his credit.

232

Lieutenant Hickman and his bride are shown cutting a 40-pound cake with a sword after their wedding at Tientsin, China, in 1948. At the right, ten years later, is Major Hickman with his wife and three children — Hilda, Robert and Christopher — in front of their home in Springfield, Va. It was the second home that Bill had built, largely with his own skilled labor in "spare time."

Bill met Christl Skoff, who is the daughter of an Austrian civil engineer, when in China. He wooed her in the old-fashioned manner before formally asking her father for her hand.

Christl saw America for the first time in 1948. Bill's parents drove from New Jersey to welcome her at San Francisco.

Like most Marine families, the Hickmans have moved every two or three years. Robert was born in 1952 while Bill was in Korea. But Christl had learned to be resourceful, and by dint of night classes Bill earned a bachelor's degree at the University of Maryland in 1958, fifteen years after he made his start at Princeton.

The "Big Bomb" at Yucca Flat

The annual atomic exercises held at Yucca Flat, Nevada, are an old story to the Marines, who send a brigade of picked troops with helicopters from Camp Pendleton every year.

The Marines are interested chiefly in testing techniques of embarkation or landing of helicopter-borne troops in an amphibious assault operation. Thus the Nevada desert is for them a simulated ocean beach, held by an enemy possessing atomic weapons.

Ever since the day of Hiroshima, when the amphibious warfare techniques of World War II were made obsolescent, the Marine Corps has been endeavoring to adapt its amphibious techniques to atomic warfare. Realizing that such concentrations of ships and landing craft as those at Iwo Jima would be suicidal against an enemy with atomic weapons, the Marines are seeking a tactical antidote in vertical helicopter landings. And the Yucca Flat exercises provide realistic tests.

The familiar mushroom cloud is shown on the opposite page as it was photographed at dawn on July 5, 1957. Two members of the 4th Marine Corps Atomic Exercise Brigade may be seen dimly beside a cactus in the foreground. Above (right) is a sunset photograph of a Marine sentry on duty near the outside perimeter of the Brigade camp. The silhouettes of spiky desert plant life appear also to be on guard. Immediately above, Marine officers are removing their gas masks a few moments after the explosion. The troops were in trenches at the time of the blast. As soon as safety permitted, Marine helicopters came forward to pick up men for a simulated amphibious assault landing' on an enemy-held beach.

The Marines Face the Future

Five years after the end of the war in Korea, the future was as clouded and uncertain for the Marines as for all other mortals in this age of "cold war." But it could never be said that the Marines weren't utilizing such new weapons as met their tactical requirements.

It was the distinction of the Marine Corps to enter World War II and the Korean War with weapons and techniques which proved in combat to be the foremost tactical innovations of both conflicts. And the Marines hope again to live up to their motto of being "America's Force in Readiness" if and when they are called to combat duty.

That call may have been heard before these words are read. Or the world may be fortunate enough to have an interlude of comparative peace. At any rate, the Marines are making it their mission to be ready either for another world war or a so-called "brush-fire war."

"The Sparrow," an air-to-air missile, has joined the Marine air-ground team. Shown above, armed with four Sparrow missiles, is a Marine F3D-2m aircraft. Below is an "Honest John" rocket of the Marine 1st Heavy Rocket Regiment at Twenty-Nine Palms, Calif.

The 30-place Sikorsky helicopter, designed to meet U. S. Army and Marine Corps requirements, is shown in the two photographs on this page, being tested near Bridgeport, Conn. It can lift twenty-six combat-equipped Marines or two jeeps. Early in 1958 the first of these aircraft were delivered to the Marines.

Men and Women of the Marines

Regardless of new weapons, the Marines realize that today, as in 1775, their true strength is found in the men of the Corps.

The sturdy soldiers of Gustavus Adolphus's army had a word for it. "The Swedes do not defend their men with walls," they said. "The Swedes defend their walls with men."

In this age it would be unjust as well as ungallant not to mention the women of the Marine Corps. The time is past when their mission was merely "to free a man to fight." Today it is recognized that they are a group of competent, educated young women who are capable of handling the most complex jobs.

As for the men, the sinews of the Corps will never grow flabby as long as "boots" go through the rugged indoctrination periods of honored tradition. Some mothers may complain of severity, but it is the soft, undisciplined man who has the poorest chance in combat.

"Miss Marine Corps" might well have been the title of Officer Candidate Florence V. King, above, if a contest had been held. Shown below are "boots" going through setting-up exercises at Parris Island.

The Marine fighting man! Out of thousands of photographs, the one above was chosen as best representing the combat Marine of the Pacific islands and Korea. Unfortunately, this young man must be nameless. We know only that he was a recent veteran of the battle for Saipan; he looks happy to be alive; and he appears to be about 18 or 19 years old. Marine enlisted men, it has been quipped, are composed "half of dead-end kids and half of youths named Percival." However true this wisecrack may be, it is a fact that the Marine Corps offers a haven equally to the young man of few opportunities and the one with a more fortunate background, who wants to prove to himself that he can "take it" along with the best.

ACKNOWLEDGMENTS

It has been truly even if tritely said that no book is ever the creation of its author alone. This rule applies with particular force to a pictorial history, which demands a variety of techniques.

As the author of the present volume, I am indebted first of all to the professional know-how of my wife, Lois H. Montross, the artist who designed the layouts. The photographs of these pages were selected from nearly five thousand in various collections, and problems of identification and reproduction arose frequently. For the solutions, I owe boundless thanks to the following organizations and individuals of Washington, D. C., all of whom made a contribution above and beyond the call of duty.

HISTORICAL BRANCH, G-3, HEADQUARTERS MARINE CORPS — Colonel Charles W. Harrison, USMC; Lieutenant Colonel John H. Magruder III, USMCR; Mrs. Elizabeth L. Tierney; Mrs. Nickey McLain; Mr. Joel D. Thacker; Mr. D. M. O'Quinlivan; Mr. John H. Marley.

PHOTOGRAPHIC SECTION, HEADQUARTERS MARINE CORPS — Captain Harley S. Hardin, USMC; Master Sergeant Warren V. Brown, USMC; Technical Sergeant Robert E. Kiser, USMC; Technical Sergeant John C. Slockbower, USMC; Staff Sergeant William F. Beasley, USMC; Staff Sergeant Edward Uminowicz, USMC; Sergeant Richard P. Thrun, USMC.

LEATHERNECK: MAGAZINE OF THE MARINES — Colonel Donald L. Dickson, USMCR; Mr. Karl A. Schuon; Mr. Lewis R. Lowery; Technical Sergeant Joseph J. Mulvihill, USMC; Staff Sergeant Woodrow W. Neel, USMC.

U. S. NAVY PHOTOGRAPHIC CENTER — Mrs. H. M. Goode.

LIBRARY OF CONGRESS — Miss Virginia Diker and Mr. Milton Kaplan.

NATIONAL ARCHIVES — Miss Josephine Motylewski.

SIGNAL CORPS, USA, STILL PICTURE BRANCH — Lieutenant Colonel H. L. Patteson, USA, and assistants.

CURATOR FOR THE NAVY DEPARTMENT — Lieutenant R. K. Hoffman, USN.

CREDITS FOR PHOTOGRAPHS AND QUOTATIONS

Abbreviations are used in the credits for photographs as follows:

Defense Department—DD; United States Army—USA; United States Navy — USN; United States Marine Corps — USMC; United States Air Force — USAF; Signal Corps — SC; Library of Congress — LC; National Archives — NA.

Facing Page 1 — USN 443340.
1. DD USMC A-352415.
2. Left to right, DD USMC A-47361, A-47357 and A-47368.
3. Right, upper to lower, DD USMC A-47364 and A-47372. Below, left to right, DD USMC A-47326, A-47371 and 47370. The quotation is from an address by Secretary of the Navy Robert N. Anderson to graduates of the Marine Corps Schools at Quantico, Va., on September 19, 1953.
4. DD USMC A-49043. The quotation is from *The Second World War* (London, 1948), by Major General J. F. C. Fuller, P. 207.
5. USMC 8251 (upper) and USMC A-49043.
6. USMC 9039-18 (upper) and DD USMC 5891.
7. USMC 5224-18 (upper) and USMC 6061.
8-9. DD USMC 7826-A.
10. DD USMC 515654 (upper) and USMC 1202.
11. DD USMC H-518 (upper) and DD USMC 519587.
12. DD USMC 515040 (upper), painted by John Clymer, and USMC 9096.
13. DD USMC H-283 (upper) and USN 421357.
14. DD USMC A-5471 (upper) and DD USMC H-420.
15. DD USMC 2269 (upper) and DD USMC 516429.
16. LC.
17. LC (upper)and DD USMC 515429.
18. USMC 6447-13 (upper) and DD USMC 515008.
19. USN 32415 (upper) and DD USMC 110974, by Sgt. Bob Cooke.
20. USMC 8619 (upper) and USMC 51566-H.
21. DD USMC 3163, by Mole and Thomas.
22. DD USMC 515478.
23. DD USMC 515746 (upper) and DD USMC 517461.
24. DD USMC A-400144.
25. DD USMC 515377. The quotation is from *Journals of the Continental Congress*, III, 348.
26. DD USMC 515321 (upper) and DD USMC 4951. The quotation is from John Adams, *Works,* III, 11-12.
27. USMC 3772-H.
28. USMC 4688.
29. USMC A-47267.
30. DD USMC 515042, by Sgt. Paul Lumbard.
31. DD USMC 515626.
32. DD USMC 4725. Painting by Col. Donald W. Dickson.
33. USN 11654 (upper) and USN Old 17407.
34. USMC 3772-H. Painting by H. C. McBarron, Jr.
35. USMC 308621 (upper) and USMC 208622. Paintings by H. C. McBarron, Jr.
36. USN 902623.
37. USN 902525.
38. USN 2137.
39. USN 8149.

40. DD USMC 515328.
41. DD USMC A-403588 (upper left), USMC H-232 (upper right) and DD USMC A-402587.
42. LC (upper) and USN Old 18170.
43. DD USMC 301136.
44. USN 902542 (upper)and USN 902649.
45. USN Old 11628 (upper), USN 902516 (middle) and USN Old 17432.
46. DD USMC 515333.
47. DD USMC 4899 (upper) and DD USMC 11353, by Sgt. Bozzie.
48. DD USMC H-556 (upper) and USN Old 2559.
49. NA SC 92660 (upper) and USN Old 12820.
50. DD USMC 515641.
51. DD USMC 515002. The quotation is from *A History of the United States Marine Corps,* by Clyde H. Metcalf (New York, 1939), 65.
52. USN Old 7913.
53. USN Old 16698.
54. USN 901024.
55. USN 901025.
56. USN 502336 (upper) and USN 902826.
57. DD USMC 301147.
58. DD USMC 515041 (upper) and DD USMC 306073.
59. DD USMC 515647 (upper) and DD USMC 515299.
60. USN Old 8313.
61. USN Old 11304 (upper) and USMC H-93.
62. LC 16718 (upper) and DD USMC 302105.
63. USN Old 17837 (upper) and USN Old 17838.
64. USN Old 4610 (upper) and DD USMC 515370.
65. USN Old 4605.
66. USN 10392 (upper) and DD USMC 4829.
67. USN Old 902368 (upper) and DD USMC 515658.
68. LC.
69. LC (upper) and USMC 4997.
70. DD USMC 308346 (upper) and DD USMC H-369.
71. DD USMC H-515334.
72. USMC H-4993 (upper) and USMC H-4952.
73. USMC H-51827 (upper) and DD USMC 515629.
74. USN Old 1084 (upper) and USN Old 11837.
75. DD USMC 4966 (upper)and USN 902575.
76. USN Old 826.
77. USN Old 804 (upper) and NA CN-6826.
78. DD USMC 515731 (upper) and DD USMC 515394.
79. DD USMC 515303 (upper) and DD USMC 513335.
80. LC (both photographs).
81. USMC 521218 (upper) and USMC 4986.
82. USMC 724.
83. USMC 4827.
84. USN Old 4443 (upper) and USN 902588.
85. USMC 515603 (upper) and LC.
86. USMC 518648 (upper) and USN Old 15711.
87. USMC H-561 (upper) and USN Old 5173.
88. NA.
89. DD USMC 517390 (upper) and DD USMC 517389.
90. USN Old 1582 (upper) and USN Old 5164.
91. DD USMC 515634 (upper) and DD USMC 515640.
92. DD USMC 516308 (upper) and DD USMC 3340-7.
93. DD USMC 515747 (upper) and NA.
94. DD USMC H-30211.
95. DD USMC H-302-5 (upper) and DD USMC 312852.
96. DD USMC 6085-12.
97. DD USMC 515261 (upper) and DD USMC 4635.
98. DD USMC 517063 (upper) and DD USMC 3090-22.
99. DD USMC H-443 (upper) and DD USMC 302177.
100. DD USMC 5224-8 (upper) and DD USMC H-428-2.
101. DD USMC 5267-427 (upper) and DD USMC 3340-52.
102. DD USMC 515274.
103. DD USMC 4941 (upper) and DD USMC 3267-58.
104. DD USMC 6085-4.
105. DD USMC 519832 (upper) and DD USMC 517089.
106. DD USMC 520242 (upper) and USMC 5012.
107. USMC Historical, no number (upper) and USMC PB-2054-32.
108. DD USMC 517396.
109. DD USMC 29477.
110. DD USMC 4921 (upper) and DD USMC 517645.
111. DD USMC 521222 (upper) and DD USMC 517757.
112. DD USMC 521249.
113. DD USMC 521248.
114. DD USMC 518249 (upper) and DD USMC 518245.
115. NA SC 4192 (upper) and NA SC 2138.
116. NA SC 15894 (upper) and NA SC 4312.
117. NA SC 11371 (upper) and NA SC 2165.
118. NA SC 12151.
119. DD USMC 518452 (upper) and DD USMC 518965.
120. DD USMC 4974 (upper) and DD USMC 4971.
121. DD USMC 519183 (upper) and DD USMC 519184.
122. NA SC 18800 (upper) and NA SC 97193.
123. DD USMC 516427 (upper) and NA SC 20705.
124. NA SC 14672 (upper) and NA SC 42736.
125. DD USMC 1318-294 (upper) and DD USMC 4973.
126. DD USMC 516421.
127. DD USMC 515645 (upper) and NA SC 89902.
128. NA SC 44327 (upper), DD USMC 515281 (lower left).
128. NA SC 44327 (upper), DD USMC 515281 (lower left) and DD USMC 515351 (lower right).
129. USMC 8984.
130. NA SC 31488.
131. NA SC 86009 (upper) and DD USMC 516426.
132. NA SC 14675 (upper) and NA SC 8364.
133. NA SC 42764 (upper) and DD USMC 516422.
134. NA SC 44931.
135. DD USMC 520331 (upper) and NA SC 30970.
136. DD USMC 520536.
137. DD USMC 521244.
138. DD USMC 515293 (upper) and DD USMC 515096.
139. DD USMC 515157. The quotation is from "The Cat With More Than Nine Lives," by Lt. Col. Robert D. Heinl, Jr., *U. S. Naval Institute Proceedings,* Vol. 80, No. 6 (June, 1954), 659.
140. DD USMC 516674 (upper) and USMC 3090-108.
141. USMC 15454 (upper) and DD USMC 518631.
142. USMC 2365-68 (upper) and USMC 3340-93.
143. USMC 2844-34 (upper) and USMC 5622-1.
144. DD USMC 307648.
145. USMC 140-20-10 (upper) and DD USMC 516301.
146. DD USMC 140-20-10 (upper) and USMC 5860-5.
147. DD USMC 312801 (upper) and USMC 5860-2.
148. USMC 4-4-5267-36 (upper) and USMC 3340-20.
149. USMC 5519-1 (upper) and USMC 5224-13.
150. USMC 516055.
151. DD USMC 55209 (upper) and USN 851723.
152. DD USMC 515159.
153. DD USMC 134687 (upper) and USMC 5067-NK2.
154. DD USMC A-16788 (upper) and DD USMC A-90932, by Sgt. C. F. Pierce.
155. USMC SC-125072. Quotation is from *The U. S. Marines and Amphibious War,* by Jeter A. Isely and Philip A. Crowl (Princeton, 1951), 36.
157. USN 16871 (upper) and USN 19930.
158. USMC 5181 (both photographs).
159. USMC 9247.
160. USN 16524 (upper), DD USMC 51370 (middle) and
160. USN 16524 (upper), DD USMC 51370 (middle) and DD USMC 50963 (lower).
161. DD USMC 53326 (upper), by Cpl. Robert Brenner, DD USMC 53444 (middle) and DD USMC 51339 (lower).
162. USMC 62632 (upper) and DD USMC, by J. F. Leopold.
163. USMC 50921 (upper), DD USMC 58869 (middle), by Sgt. Diet, and USN 51633 (lower).
164. DD USMC 63478.
165. DD USMC 63495 (upper) and DD USMC 64019.
166. DD USMC 57685 (upper) and USN 216218.
167. DD USMC 116412 (upper), by Johnson, and USN 57976.
168. USMC 126420 (upper)and USN 432752.
169. USN 216608 (upper) and USN 58387.

170. USN 234712 (upper), DD USMC 84019 (lower left), by Cpl. A. Robertson, and USN 234719 (lower right).
171. USN 238187 (upper left), USN 238043 (upper right), and USN 238190.
172. USN 238994 (upper) and USN 239020.
173. USN 237568 (upper) and USN 249295.
174. DD USMC 94986 (upper), by Sgt. J. D. Wasden, and USN 59496.
175. DD USMC 95367 (upper), by Pvt. Bob Bailey, and USN 217191.
176. USN 309193 (upper) and DD USMC 111688 (middle), by B. Campbell, and DD USMC 110100, by Cpl. Schwartz.
177. USN 304865 (upper) and DD USMC 62705, by Capt. O'Sheel.
178. DD USMC 1109922 (upper), by T/Sgt. B. Ferneyhough, DD USMC 110250 (middle), by Dreyfuss, and USN 485557.
179. USN 69199 (upper), DD USMC 111993 (middle), by Pvt. Charles Jones, and DD USMC 1111689 (lower), by Bob Campbell.
180. USN 329038 (upper) and DD USMC 119812, by Giffin.
181. USMC 126456 (upper), by Cpl. W. C. Beall, and USN 329090.
182. DD USMC 123170 (upper), by Sgt. W. F. Kleine, DD USMC 123331 (middle), by Sgt. Kleine, and DD USMC 120267 (lower), by Pvt. Bob Bailey.
183. DD USMC 8325011.
184. DD USMC A-41924 (upper) and DD USMC A-46207, by Sgt. Thomas.
185. USN 408458. Quotation is from P. 6-7 of Cavalry of the Sky, by Lynn Montross (New York, 1954).
186. DD USMC A-119280 (upper), by Sgt. Myers, and DD USMC A-119286, by Capt. Reed.
187. DD USMC A1788, by Sgt. F. J. Hotman.
188. DD USMC 82173 (upper), by Sgt. F. C. Kerr, and DD USMC A-31200, by Cpl. R. J. Laitinen.
189. USN 446192 (upper) and DD USMC A-131200, by T/Sgt. Vance Jobe.
190. DD USMC A-3189 (upper) and DD USMC A-3191, both by S/Sgt. W. W. Frank.
191. DD USMC A-2739 (upper), by Sgt. F. C. Kerr, and DD USMC A-3704, by Cpl. R. J. Laitinen.
192. DD USMC A-3228 (upper) and USA SC 350926.
193. DD USMC A-3386 (upper), by Sgt. J. N. Babyak, and SC 349149.
194. Courtesy of Lt. Gen. Edward A. Craig, USMC (Ret.)
195. DD USMC A-4315 (upper) and USN 241335.
196. DD USMC A-130507 (upper), by S/Sgt. E. D. Barnum, and DD USMC A-5377.
197. DD USMC A-4839 (upper) and DD USMC A-5388.
198. DD USMC A-5438 (upper) and DD USMC A-5464, both by Sgt. F. C. Kerr.
199. DD USMC A-5434 (upper), by Sgt. F. C. Kerr, DD USMC A-4866 (middle) and DD USMC A-5386 (lower), by McDonald.
200. DD USMC A-4854 (upper) and DD USMC A-5357, both by Sgt. F. C. Kerr.
201. DD USMC A-5677 (upper), DD USMC A-5676 (middle), by Cpl. L. V. Snyder, and DD USMC A-159017, by M/Sgt. R. E. Gland.
202. USN no number (upper) and (lower), courtesy of Sgt. James Ramp.
203. DD USMC A-156323 (upper), by T/Sgt. J. W. Helms, and USN 423911.
204. DD USMC A-6869 (upper), by Pfc. C. T. Wehner, and DD USMC A-9766, by Sgt. Uthe.
205. DD USMC A-6720 (upper), DD USMC A-6754 (middle) and DD USMC A-7383 (lower), all by Pfc. C. T. Wehner.
206. DD USMC A-130949, by S/Sgt. Ed. Barnum. Quotation is from The Sea War in Korea, by Commanders Malcolm W. Cagle, USN, and Frank A. Manson, USN (U. S. Naval Institute, 1957), 309.
207. DD USMC A-155692 (upper) by Sgt. Early, DD USMC A-8370 (middle) and DD USMC A-156992, by Sgt. Thomas Towey.
208. USN 443547 (upper) and DD USMC A-159193, by M/Sgt. Frank W. Sewell.
209. USN 446908 (upper) and DD USMC A-158912, by S/Sgt. R. H. Mosier.
210. DD USMC A-159621 (upper), by M/Sgt. R. E. Olund, DD USMC A-123111 (middle) and DD USMC A-165437 (lower), by S/Sgt. E. J. Scullin.
211. DD USMC A-166437, by M/Sgt. J. S. Galloway.
212. DD USMC A-162801 (upper), by M/Sgt. J. S. Galloway, and DD USMC A-171018, by Sgt. C. Chokakis.
213. DD USMC A-134109 (upper), DD USMC A-168980, by Cpl. E. E. Beals.
214. DD USMC A-164148, by S/Sgt. E. Scullin.
215. DD USMC A-164861 (upper), by S/Sgt. M. Riley, DD USMC A-164148.
216. DD USMC A-164861 (upper), by Sgt. W. J. Zurheide, and DD USMC A-156728, by T/Sgt. V. Murdutt.
217. USN 441110 (upper) and DD USMC A-8504.
218 and 219. Courtesy of Leatherneck Magazine, by S/Sgt. Woodrow W. Neel.
220. DD USMC 25767 (upper) and DD USMC 308924, by T/Sgt. Skhymba.
221. USMC 8783-62 (upper) and USMC 8783-63.
222. DD USMC A-65926 (upper), by Cpl. Coppa, and DD USMC A-66582, by Cpl. E. T. Olson.
223. DD USMC A-65176 (upper), by Pfc. K. Schultz, and USN 473681.
224. DD USMC A-600124 (upper) and DD USMC 313746, by S/Sgt. A. Waddington.
225. DD USMC 313746, by S/Sgt. Waddington.
226. DD USMC 4604 (upper) and DD USMC 307278.
227. USMC 12998 (upper) and USMC no number. Quotation is from Page 50 of an unpublished manuscript, History of the United States Marine Band, by Joel D. Thacker, in the archives of the Historical Branch, G-3, Headquarters Marine Corps.
228. DD USMC 12444B (upper left) DD USMC 306428 (middle) by M/Sgt. J. G. Daly, DD USMC A-42546 (upper right) and photo by Leatherneck (lower.)
229. DD USMC A-46470 (upper left), by Lt. R. E. Westmoreland, DD USMC A-402599 (upper right) and photo by Leatherneck (lower).
230. DD USMC A-49058 (upper), by Sgt. E. H. Mai, DD USMC A-402830 (middle) and DD USMC A-179617 (lower).
231. DD USMC A-179294 (upper), by Pfc. J. L. Thomas, and DD USMC A-400463, by Cpl. D. M. Sutton.
232. Snapshots enlarged by Sgt. Richard P. Thrun.
233. USMC no number (upper) and DD USMC A-406551 by Sgt. Richard P. Thrun.
234. DD USMC A-352715.
235. DD USMC A-352734 (upper) and DD A-352702.
236. DD USMC A-199017 (upper) and DD USMC A-361171.
237. DD USMC A-49993 (upper) and DD USMC A-401914.
238. USMC no number (upper) and SS USMC 18160.
239. USN 475139.

DATE DUE

MM 23, 2003	
	PRINTED IN U.S.A.

DEMCO NO 295